SABINA SPENCER PHD is a pioneer in the field of Global Leadership Development. For the past two decades she has been working in the areas of strategic change and inspirational leadership with some of the world's largest corporations.

Praise for *The Heart of Leadership*:

'Here is a book that develops some important antidotes to the complexities and pressures of the twenty-first century. Sabina Spencer provides solid guidance to anyone who chooses to take leadership in the years ahead.' John Adams PhD, Professor and Chair, Organizational Systems PhD Program, Saybrook Graduate School

'An invaluable resource guide and an excellent synthesis of diverse leadership models, skills and practices . . . an essential book for our times!' Angeles Arrien PhD, author of *The Four-Fold Way* and *Signs of Life*

'An essential guide to the distribution of leadership throughout an organisation. This book provides a common-sense framework for the necessary and constant pursuit of success and excellence.' David Brown, Vice President, Sabre Inc.

'Sabina issues an evocative and heartfelt call to leaders who are seeking to make a difference in these challenging times. She invites us to undertake the important work that is needed to create a sustainable future, not only for ourselves, but for future generations.' Juanita Brown PhD, Co-founder, The World Café

'A unique and holistic perspective on leadership full of rich insights for both our professional and personal lives . . . an inspirational guide for everybody who wishes to make a *real* difference in today's rapidly changing world.' Stig Eriksson, Vice President, 3M

'Leaders often leave their hearts outside the office door as they struggle to come to terms with ever-changing demands and challenges. This inspiring book offers practical steps to develop a more authentic and sustainable leadership approach.' Sandy Fiechtner, Director Human Resources, Pfizer Inc

'Sabina Spencer's entrancing book will guide, support and challenge the reader with globally gathered insight, passion and a reassuring twinkle in the eye.' Phil Hodgson, Director of Leadership Programmes, Ashridge Management College and author of *The Future of Leadership* and *Relax, It's Only Uncertainty*

'One of the year's most important leadership books . . . an extraordinary collection of timeless lessons for leaders, managers and CEOs.' Richard J. Leider, Founder of The Inventure Group and author of *Repacking Your Bags* and *Whistle Why You Work*

'*The Heart of Leadership* provides powerful insights into both the "why" and "how" of harnessing the full potential of employees to achieve the organisation's and their own personal goals. This book is not just about leadership in organisations but about understanding and enhancing relationships in our daily life.' Doug Mitchell, Business Director, Transportation Business, Europe and EEMENA 3M UK

'Sabina Spencer has written a wise and inspiring book that challenges us to recognise the transformative power of authenticity and love in the world today. This book is vitally important to our understanding of how the inner life of mind and spirit affects relationships and the fate of the Earth. It is essential reading for anyone interested in developing effective, compassionate leadership.' Frances Vaughan, author of *Shadows of the Sacred*

The Heart of Leadership

Unlock your inner wisdom and inspire others

Sabina Spencer

RIDER
London . Sydney . Auckland . Johannesburg

1 3 5 7 9 10 8 6 4 2

First published in 2004 by Rider,
an imprint of Ebury Press, Random House,
20 Vauxhall Bridge Road, London SW1V 2SA

Random House Australia (Pty) Limited
20 Alfred Street, Milsons Point, Sydney,
New South Wales 2061, Australia

Random House New Zealand Limited
18 Poland Road, Glenfield,
Auckland 10, New Zealand

Random House South Africa (Pty) Limited
Endulini, 5A Jubilee Road,
Parktown 2193, South Africa

The Random House Group Limited Reg. No. 954009

Papers used by Rider are natural, recyclable products made from wood grown in sustainable forests.

Typeset by Palimpsest Book Production Limited, Polmont, Stirlingshire
Printed and bound in Great Britain by Mackays of Chatham plc, Kent

A CIP catalogue record for this book
is available from the British Library

ISBN 1-8441-3232-3

To My Soul Partner

My sincere gratitude for your
Strength,
Trust,
Inspiration and
Guidance.
You taught me what it means to be real.

To
Mystery, Magic
and
Miracles

CONTENTS

Part One: The Relationship Age

1 The Invitation 3
2 The 'Buck' Starts Here 10
3 The Soft Stuff is Really the Hard Stuff 30
4 Power and the 'F' Word 44
5 Living with Energy 57

Part Two: The Seven Keys

6 Establishing Security 65
7 Generating Passion 78
8 Sharing Power 91
9 Inspiring Love 109
10 Voicing Truth 128
11 Trusting Intuition 151
12 Honouring the Mystery 172

Part Three: Four-Dimensional Leadership

13 Four-Dimensional Leadership 191
14 Leading with Intention 208

References and Further Reading 217
Acknowledgements 221
Index 224

Part One

THE RELATIONSHIP AGE

THE INVITATION

Destiny is not already made,
Destiny is what we are making.
Hazrat Inayat Khan

The Relationship Age

WITH EVERYTHING THAT HAS happened already in these early years of the twenty-first century, now is the perfect time to deeply question the leadership assumptions that have led us to where we are today. As we move more fully into this new millennium we have a tremendous chance to choose more consciously a future for ourselves that is different from the past.

We are passing through a time of major struggles and of great potential, a time for breaking through patterns of behaviour that no longer add value and that keep us stuck in the ways of the past. These patterns, if allowed to continue, will take us into an increasingly soulless existence, where feelings of isolation and burnout become commonplace, and both our work and our relationships cease to fulfil and sustain us.

It is a time when people all over the world are waking up to the fact that our societies and institutions can no longer operate effectively with assumptions and beliefs designed for an age long gone. These old ways of thinking cause us to hold on to stability, hierarchical authority, outer security, ethnic uniformity and strong boundaries between disciplines, nations and ideologies. Today, things are different. In our increasingly complex world, change can no longer be viewed as an event, with a beginning, middle and an end, to be controlled at will. Rather, it has to be seen as a self-generating process, nudging us ever more swiftly in the direction of a whole new way of living and working together as a global society.

The Industrial Age of the 1940s, 50s, and 60s, with its focus on the manufacture of goods and continued scientific development, led to significant advances in technology. As consumerism increased in the West, we witnessed the introduction of sophisticated machines that changed the world and the way we live. It was the spawning of the Information Age, a time when computer technology began to blow wide open the traditional channels of power and communication, and shifted the rules of the game in virtually every facet of the Western way.

During the second half of the twentieth century we saw the birth of the debtor society, the creation of global economies and radical changes in the ways families live together and children learn. People everywhere became more mobile, the media's impact on influencing our perspectives of reality increased beyond belief and business emerged as the institution best positioned to lead us into a global reality. Its influence on the dissolution of traditional boundaries and the creation of market economies has shown us the tremendous power that is shaping our future.

However, the Information Age, like its predecessor, is merely the facilitator to the next era of our development as a human family. It has allowed us to open our eyes to a whole new worldview. The Internet, email, video conferencing, CNN and mobile phones are busy connecting us in every way imaginable, showing us that we are not as distant or as different from one another as we may have thought. Products like Levi Jeans, Coca-Cola, Sony television, 3M's yellow sticky Post-it notes and Nike trainers, once only available in 'developed' countries, can now be found virtually everywhere we go. The Global Giants have penetrated every corner of the world and, with technology as their greatest ally, have led us from the Information Age slap-bang into the *Relationship Age*.

It seems, however, given the recent crises in corporate confidence and the war in Iraq in 2003, that the evolution of a leadership consciousness consistent with this age of interconnection is lagging behind the systems and technology that are weaving us all together. Many of us are demanding more integrity and more transparency. People want recognition that they are not simply cogs in a vast machine, to be used up and replaced. Wealth and success are no longer enough for many as the search for greater fulfilment from life and work becomes paramount.

We are hungry for something different, something new. We want a leadership orientation that is rooted in deeper, more spiritual values and that takes into account the full spectrum of the human experience. We want truth, authenticity and the recognition that self-interest is no longer acceptable when it is at the cost of the common good. People want those in leadership roles to place the care for the collective above (or at the very least on a par with) their own personal gain. Their legitimacy will be seriously challenged if they fail to value the well-being of every individual within their sphere of influence irrespective of wealth and position.

Unanswered Questions

The implications of this shift are more far-reaching than we can yet imagine. With the growing recognition that we are entering the *Relationship Age*, profound questions are being raised about the way we live together on what the late Carl Sagan referred to as 'this pale blue dot' – a small planet with finite resources and protected by a thin layer of gas that is becoming increasingly vulnerable.

Some of the questions being asked are deeply personal and have been echoed by philosophers and mystics throughout the ages. These questions are about life's meaning and our relationship to our soul's purpose, about spirituality, about life and death, about balance and success and about our relationship to the Earth and each other.

There are also broader questions that ask us to examine our relationships as a collective. What are the roles of the nation state, big business and the United Nations in a global society? What can we do to monitor the use of non-renewable resources, and address issues of population, human rights, health, ethics and security in a world where the boundaries are becoming more permeable and blurry? Still others engage us in another level of enquiry. They are designed to help us clarify the nature of leadership that will take us forward, as we grapple with increasing levels of complexity and paradox.

Over the past few years, it has become clear that one of the biggest challenges facing many organisations and governments is an absence of leadership breadth and depth. That is to say, a shortage of people who have the capacity to exercise leadership in a global reality. Companies are realising that they need a set of very different leadership competencies in a world that is so clearly interconnected. They also recognise that they are operating in an environment where the sustainability of high-quality relationships based on truth and integrity is critical to securing competitive advantage. Today, price, product and service are no longer enough to earn the status of preferred supplier. If an organisation wants to retain its high-potential people, it will have to make a significant investment in the kind of leadership orientation that will inspire such talent to remain with it.

If we focus on the public arena, we also discover that people are finding it harder to identify suitable candidates to hold public office. Quality people, who they believe have the potential and integrity to provide leadership for their institutions, communities and societies, are hard to find. In fact, it is clear that we are facing a crisis of leadership throughout the world today, as we transition into this next era.

Leadership in the *Relationship Age* must be rooted in a set of fundamental assumptions that are very different from those that served a world that was a collection of discrete, independent territories. It was a world where the language of our corporations and governments was made up of words such as 'divisions', 'departments', 'sections', 'levels' and 'units' – words that so clearly promote separation. It was a different world from today's. Leaders can no longer afford to be all-knowing, operating with a divide-and-conquer mentality, focusing their energies on protecting their fiefdoms, controlling resources, addressing short-term needs and maintaining firm boundaries – and yet too many still do. We all know who they are.

With today's rapidly changing conditions, such a style of leadership suppresses talent and limits the growth potential of those enterprises and individuals that continue to reward it. The emerging leadership orientation must recognise that the world is a single integrated system, invisible threads woven together in an intricate web of relationships that result in high levels of economic and environmental interdependency. Words like 'networks', 'alliances', 'communities', 'partnerships' and 'teams' are helping to shape the language of connectedness. But words are only the beginning. Those who take on the new leadership roles will have to learn to walk the talk or their credibility will be short-lived.

Leadership in an age of connection can no longer afford to focus *solely* on strategy, structure and concrete results. The very essence of what is emerging demands attention to a set of values that embrace the spiritual and emotional dimensions of human existence – in other words the *heart* and *soul* of our everyday living. The new leadership has to integrate these aspects of our humanity and provide the inspiration and sense of meaning needed to thrive in a global society, otherwise it will falter.

The Invitation

What you will find in the pages that follow are some new ideas and some ancient truths. All of this is given as food for thought, to provide some insight into the personal challenges and opportunities that face each of us who chooses to fully engage in this process of fundamental transformation.

This book presents a philosophy of leadership that integrates the mental, physical, spiritual and emotional dimensions, providing a new understanding for what it means to live with integrity. It's about reclaiming our soul's authority and the energy that ignites our curiosity, our courage, our compassion and our creativity. *The Heart of Leadership* provides the keys to unlock the true essence of authentic power that shines from the inside out. The concepts challenge us to reach for the highest in ourselves in the service of something greater. This is a book about the soul's search for love and fulfilment in the work that we do and the people we meet. And it's about the soft stuff that inspires excellence and empowers us to be the very best we can be right here and right now.

The Heart of Leadership is an invitation to take personal

authorship for creating new ways of living and leading that are very different from the past. *Part One* lays the groundwork for a new orientation to leadership, describing how we are moving into an age of interconnection. These chapters describe the shift in mind-set needed to make sense of all the changes that are happening. They detail the importance of reclaiming the 'softer' (but often harder to handle) qualities of the human experience, if we are to be effective in this new era.

Part Two provides insight into the Seven Keys to Authentic Power. These Keys open the doors that free the energy of the human spirit, and allow us to reclaim our role in providing inspirational leadership. Each Key challenges us to release the energy that is held back by our fears. There are descriptions of the implications on personal, organisational and global levels of every Key, and the leadership capabilities attributed to each. For some of us certain Keys will be more challenging than others, depending on our life experiences and where we have focused our life energies.

Part Three provides a framework for global leadership integrating the Seven Keys with the four dimensions of mind, body, spirit and emotions. It describes four leadership archetypes, the Transformer, Map Maker, Connector and Navigator. To be fully effective we need all of these developed within ourselves. We also need them represented in a healthy combination in the outside world if we are to redress existing imbalances and create a sustainable future.

The fifth dimension and the 'Master Key' are introduced in the last chapter. Sourcing our lives from our soul's intention and not simply addressing the needs of our egos is the ultimate challenge. With this awareness our lives are transformed, and we find within ourselves the unconditional love that allows us to serve in ways that are inspirational and enriching to the world around us.

The words on these pages apply whether we work in organisations or operate independently. If we want a world that is different from the one we live in today, then each of us needs to take a good look inside, and reconnect to the parts of ourselves that know how to make this happen. We have to release the old fears that hold us back from being fully alive in the moment.

It's time for us all to turn our lights back up to full beam. The world needs us to actively engage in the transformation of leadership that supports a global society. There's a growing urgency to weave all the disparate threads together in ways that secure a healthy future for ourselves and the generations that follow. It's unreasonable to leave this to a few men and women. They will only fail us.

There is no greater gift that we can give to the world than the loving acceptance of our own soul's journey. That's all it takes and that's what it takes. The choice is ours, to continue along the path of the past, or accept the invitation to engage in the definition of leadership for the *Relationship Age*. The journey through these pages provides an opportunity for each of us to release any outdated patterns and actively participate in shaping our collective destiny. Surely it's too good an invitation to miss, because to leave this responsibility in the hands of 'somebody else' would certainly be a mistake; after all, isn't the future of our world everybody's business?

2 □

THE 'BUCK' STARTS HERE

The moment we relinquish our need to find
someone else to give us safety and security,
we discover we already have it!
Gareth Brown

IF WE CHOOSE TO accept the invitation and take our part in shaping the nature of leadership in the *Relationship Age*, we will need to examine the mindsets that influence our thoughts, feelings and behaviour. When we look at the world through global glasses there is no 'there' there anymore, only here and only now! It used to be so easy to say it's not happening here, it's happening 'over "there",' when we heard news that disturbed us about another country, another family, another company, another race, religion or community. It was a wonderful way to think it was all somebody else's responsibility.

Today, it's hard to deny that we're living in a global society and that right now we are facing major challenges on the physical, mental, spiritual and emotional dimensions that are affecting each and every one of us. These include global warming, the spread of diseases, increasing violence, the unequal distribution of wealth, the abuse of power and the challenging of religious dogma. Issues of leadership lie at the heart of all these and are clearly central to the economic instability that has arisen as a result of the recent corporate scandals and the crisis with Iraq.

Images of September 11 2001 are fixed in our minds forever and are vivid reminders of both our interconnectedness and our vulnerability. It was a shocking realisation to discover that such symbols of extraordinary economic strength can be wiped out in minutes, as we continue to destroy each other in the most hideous ways. The message is clear – unless we get our collective act together, the future may well become a thing of the past!

Challenges like this transcend the boundaries of businesses, governments and religion, and if allowed to continue unabated, are likely to have disastrous consequences. What is needed is a change of leadership consciousness, a different way of 'seeing and being' in the world, rather than another set of skills and traits. We need to focus on what connects us as well as what separates us and learn to explore how we can value our differences, seeing them as complementary rather than as a cause for conflict. We need to let go of a belief in scarcity and decide that there really is enough to go round, if only we are willing to share. And we need to change our fundamental assumption, as a human society, from 'survival of the fittest' to 'if somebody loses then nobody wins'.

Ending the Blame Game

When things aren't going well we often look outside ourselves to find out who or what we can blame for what's not working in our lives. Sometimes it's our job, our partners, our in-laws, our neighbours or the dog! Just think for a moment about how many times you have felt grumpy for a few days, looked for all the reasons outside yourself why, and then woken up one morning feeling fine. In the meantime the only thing that's changed is your perspective and your attitude.

For a lot of us, our personality's default setting is to externalise the source of our problems. It's the way we've been educated. We blame others rather than exploring how our own thinking may be creating the results we are getting in our lives. It's a difficult concept to grasp, but think of the changes we could make if we believed the words of Robert Fritz, that 'we are the predominant creative force in our own lives'.

So how do we break this trend of blame and recognise that we're the ones responsible for repeating our old patterns, and that equally we can become the architects of new experiences for ourselves? Where do these habit patterns come from in the first place and what is the cost of maintaining them in relation to claiming our authentic leadership power?

Changing our Minds

As long as we hold on to our current beliefs, we will behave in the same ways and continue to get the same results. In order to stop playing the blame game and take back responsibility, we must become conscious of the beliefs that are creating our experience of reality. In the words of Wayne Dyer, 'we'll see it when we believe it'. A twist on the old adage, yet a powerful reminder of how our beliefs determine our perspective.

With the pressure on being externally focused, many of us rarely take enough time to venture inwards and examine the assumptions, beliefs and values that are influencing our thoughts and shaping our everyday experiences. In seminars we often ask participants how much time they take by themselves both reflecting upon and consciously directing the course of their life. Few take an hour a day, some admit to an hour a week, others only take the time when on vacation! Yet until we do, nothing is going to change very much. Many of us tell ourselves that there is not enough time for that kind of dreaming. The truth is we simply don't make it a priority

Research suggests that we have thousands of thoughts a day and the majority are the same ones we had the day before. John D. Adams, author of *Thinking Today as if Tomorrow Mattered: The Rise of a Sustainable Consciousness*, describes it this way: 'This repetitious thinking represents tremendous reinforcement of the status quo. If we actually do choose a different future, we must first become aware of how our present beliefs and values are actually largely responsible for creating our everyday experiences. Then, we have the ability to change how we are thinking, how we are behaving, and ultimately, the experiences we can expect to have.'

If we put all this in a nutshell, it says, quite simply, that until we become more aware of the unconscious patterns that are responsible for the choices we are making in how we live our lives, we can't expect things to change very much. For a lot of us the first step is to become conscious of being conscious. We have to turn inwards and reconnect to a deeper way of knowing. After a lifetime of programming this may not be as easy as it sounds.

In order to simplify this notion, Table 1 introduces four different

EVOLVING MINDSETS

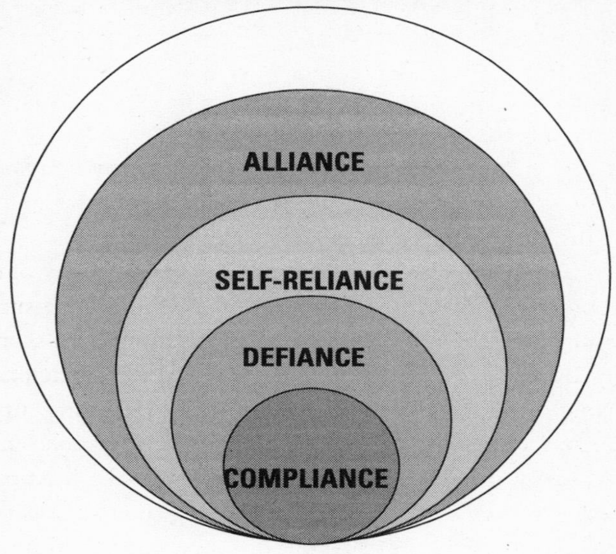

Mindset	**COMPLIANCE**	**DEFIANCE**	**SELF-RELIANCE**	**ALLIANCE**
Basis of relationships	Dependence	Counter-dependence	Independence	Inter-dependence
Values	Security Conformity	Freedom Non-conformity	Autonomy Diversity	Contribution Unity
Underlying Question	How do I fit in?	How do I break out?	How do I make a difference?	How do I serve?
Motivation	To belong	To be different	To achieve	To add value
Core Belief	We are separate	I am unique	I am alone	We're connected
Orientation to power	Externalised	Externalised	Internalised Personal Will	Internalised Divine Will
Nature of Leadership	Paternalistic Hierarchical	Rebellious	Entrepreneurial	Inspirational
Fundamental Assumption	Survival of the Fittest	Divide and Conquer	In the grand scheme I matter	If somebody loses, nobody wins

mindsets, with the characteristics of individuals and organisations that express them. The leadership consciousness and the nature of relationships are significantly different in each of these mindsets, moving from *dependence* in the *Compliance* mindset to *interdependence* in the *Alliance* mindset.

Compliance

When we are young we are taught to develop a mindset of *compliance*, promoting relationships of *dependence*, because we are driven by our basic needs for security and belonging. In our early years it's important to have a set of values that support these needs. We look to our parents and other authority figures to help us feel safe, as we seek to address the question: '*How do I fit in?*'

This mindset emphasises the physical side of life and is rooted in the beliefs that we are all separate, that power lies outside us and that people need to be controlled. It encourages us to look to others for leadership and approval, and to value comfort and consistency above change and creativity. The compliance orientation leads us to suppress our soul's authority and build strong ego identities in order to survive.

As we mature it is important that we develop our own beliefs that come from our personal experiences, letting go of those with which we have been programmed. When we hold on to compliance as our only mindset, we adopt one of two possible life positions, which significantly influence our leadership capacity. In the first case, we continue to look outside ourselves for direction, giving away our authentic leadership power and our right to be uniquely who we are. In the second case, we make the acquisition of wealth and the responsibility for others our ambition, believing that the more resources we control, the more powerful and secure we are. The assumption of survival of the fittest perpetuates this view of life, and in the end it becomes a self-fulfilling prophecy. Everyone competes for, and acquires, what are believed to be scarce resources.

The style of leadership that grows out of this assumption promotes competition, conformity and top-down control. People in positions of power and authority ensure compliance to a set of beliefs and behaviours that maintain order and dependence. Some degree of this is needed to protect us, provide us with a sense of belonging and ensure our survival. When this is overdone, such a mindset not only excludes those with different beliefs, but the leadership that emerges becomes self-serving and self-limiting.

> John had just taken up the appointment as the managing director of a five-thousand-person company. It was a subsidiary of the parent organisation, to which he would return at a more senior position, if he performed well in his new role. The culture of the country and the way work got done was different to what he was used to. Instead of taking time to understand and discover how he could best provide leadership to these people, he assumed that they would simply do as they were told, because after all that was what he did. He made this expectation very clear in one of his first meetings with his new management team when he said, 'I do what my boss tells me, it's as simple as that – he's the one punching my ticket!'

A large part of society, and the economic models that support it, reinforces such a mindset. Those in leadership roles in certain organisations and public offices unconsciously encourage beliefs that promote fear, powerlessness and dependency. In many institutions the leaders are doing nothing more than playing the role of controlling and protective parents. They set boundaries and promote the safety mechanisms to stop those they perceive as less capable from making the 'wrong' choices.

Some of these behaviours, although well intentioned, when overused in today's society lead to varying levels of dysfunction. A leadership orientation that reinforces a predominant compliance mindset inhibits risk-taking, represses creativity, promotes cultural uniformity and discourages individual initiative.

In organisations that rely *heavily* on compliance, there is little tolerance for mistakes and experimentation, people are politically polite and a great deal of energy is used to maintain internal consistency. Processes promote compliance rather than encourage autonomy, and there is usually plenty of micro-management. Cost management becomes the driving force, and return on shareholder value becomes the organisation's sole 'reason for being'. A strong emphasis on short-term results leaves little room for relationship building, and the expression of emotion is not a valued part of doing business. The result is that the people side of work is sadly lacking and the light of the human spirit is kept in the shadows.

With an absence of relationship skills, people in these organisations lack the needed behaviours to ensure a clear customer (community) orientation. Despite their best intentions and efforts, the demands for internal compliance and the lack of empowerment at the interface with the outside world seem like an uphill struggle. The talk is sweet but the behaviours don't match. As a result, the customers feel undervalued, finding it difficult to access the people who can make decisions and meet their needs. Faceless organisations and endless telephone push-button instructions with musical interludes characterise these businesses.

When this mindset is predominant the net effect is an enormous onus of accountability on 'those at the top' to get things right. So leaders become even more directive in order to prevent loss of control. Often, unable to see how some of their beliefs and assumptions about leadership may be outdated, they become consumed by inordinate levels of responsibility.

Defiance

The second of these four mindsets, *defiance*, is driven by our need to find our unique identities. In doing so we often form relationships that have a flavour of *counterdependence* as we attempt to redefine ourselves. We are looking for the answer to the question: '*How do I break out?*'

At this point of our development we delight in pushing against authority figures in order to shake off the beliefs and values that now feel like a straitjacket. Instead of providing a sense of security the beliefs and the behaviours that once kept us 'safe' now feel like they imprison us!

The defiance mindset, like compliance, also perpetuates the assumption of survival of the fittest, with a focus primarily on the physical world and the idea of separateness. Some of the beliefs about 'who knows best what's good for me' change significantly. Here the belief that if I want control over my life I have to take it from *them* replaces the willingness to comply with authority. It is a classic struggle for power yet it is still based on the notion of a 'them and us' and a 'one up, one down' philosophy.

This period of rebelliousness is an essential part of the growth process en route to claiming our true leadership potential. Still seeing the 'real' power as being outside ourselves, we create relationships that are counterdependent. This is where we confront or rebel against those in authority, or those who threaten us in our attempt to cut loose from the established order.

In the broader society, this defiance mindset gets played out in the formation of gangs and cliques. With a desire to be unique and break free of conformity, teenagers (and others) simply create a new set of behaviours that ironically become their own set of norms for ensuring compliance. In the world at large, we see this when rebel forces with an alternative ideology oust or attempt to overthrow those in power.

In organisations where the defiance mindset is rife, there is open questioning and challenging of the credibility of the existing leadership. People defy control and openly challenge the policies, procedures and norms that they feel are outdated or restrictive. Emotions run high as people drive to destabilise the status quo. Open conflict and tensions exist between key players and respect for difference gets lost in the struggle for power. As a result the organisation begins to fragment into different camps, such as those who want to comply and those who want to do it their way.

Effective leadership at this point channels this powerful energy and focuses it on productive outcomes. Unfortunately in a lot of cases where fear of loss of control dominates, so-called troublemakers are shut down or put into places where they can do the least harm.

> George was a young manager at a chemical plant. He was full of bright ideas and was different from his peers. Some saw him as a bit of a rebel. Others recognised he had a brilliant mind and encouraged him to speak out, knowing his heart was in the right place. One day a senior manager who was unfamiliar with George's style and behaviour visited the plant. During a presentation some questions were asked and George's response was challenging and a little threatening to the more traditional thinking of the visitor. As the senior manager left, he turned to the plant director and told him that he didn't want to see George on any high-potential list.

George's behaviour is typical of someone in the defiance mindset confronting someone with a strong attachment to compliance. Individuals who get stuck in this mindset, and don't see it as a step in an ongoing process of autonomy, can become belligerent, angry people. They end up spending their energy 'fighting' against a perceived enemy, unwilling to look inside themselves and adopt a more reasoned approach.

Self-Reliance

The third mindset in this evolutionary journey is *self-reliance*, and the nature of the resulting relationships promotes *independence*. When we take this next step towards claiming our authentic leadership power, we find ourselves engaged in a significant process of re-evaluation. In letting go of the need to push against authority, we move into a period of soul-searching to find the answer to the question: '*How do I make a difference?*'

Once we believe in our ability to bring something unique to the world, we become more assertive of our wants and needs. We turn inward, beginning a journey to discover a deeper sense of destiny. We intuitively know there has to be more to life than meets the eye and we find the courage to take the risks that will free us from attachment to the 'shoulds' of our prior existence. Although sometimes a hugely challenging experience, it is at this stage we accept accountability for our thoughts, feelings and actions as we establish our own value and belief structure.

> Sandra had always known she wanted to be a pilot but her upbringing had led her to believe that this was a man's job. For a while she studied psychology but she was much more interested in aeroplanes. She became more miserable as time went on and although she knew she risked significant disapproval from her parents she decided to follow her heart's desire. At first they were very unsupportive and had little belief in her ever fulfilling her dream. They tried to discourage her from making the change and only focused on the downside of such a choice.
>
> She spoke of how she struggled for months, torn between what she thought she 'should' do and what she so wanted to do. But in the end she said, 'I had to take responsibility for my own choices and believe in myself, otherwise I would spend my life resenting them.' After coming to terms with the lack of acceptance by her family, she knew what she had to do. She knew what gave her life meaning even if it meant disappointing others.

Like many of us she discovered that freedom is not found from complying with others' beliefs, it comes from letting go of the need for outside approval and making the commitment to discover our unique purpose.

This mindset also places less emphasis on physical possessions and more on the idea of a lifelong journey of learning. The motivation towards growth and autonomy, both intellectually and spiritually, becomes the goal when we adopt this way of thinking. Physical survival is no longer the primary driver. Instead, curiosity and self-expression become highly valued in every aspect of life. The need for openness and emotional availability in relationships, first with the self and then with others, becomes a core value. Once we reach this stage of self-reliance, we let go of the need to make others responsible for our lives and we seize the leadership responsibility for our 'Self'.

We recognise that we have the power to transform our own consciousness. We challenge our assumptions, and change those beliefs that don't support our creative nature, allowing us to engage in sharing the responsibility for the way things are. As we shift away from a material focus, towards one that values and integrates the spiritual and emotional aspects, we move into a whole new orientation to leadership. It is here we begin to recognise that we are not really separate but rather we are profoundly connected to all those around us.

The nature of leadership in a mindset of self-reliance encourages us to be autonomous and self-directed, accepting the authority for our lives. With a strong value on freedom of expression, we encourage others to speak their minds, assert their wants, be genuine in their emotional expression and to take their power. By connecting to our deeper spiritual roots we respect the rights of others to be guided by theirs.

> Andy had a quiet personality and didn't walk the corridors too often, preferring to stay in his office. He was well liked by his peers. His team, however, was a little unsure of him at first because he had taken the place of a more extroverted manager who was both expressive and directive. As time went on they began to warm to him, although they found this change in style a little alarming. Andy believed in helping people to help themselves. When they came in to see him to get an answer to a problem the way they had with his predecessor, he would begin asking them questions. Some of them thought his behaviour was a little manipulative at first. They believed that he knew the 'right' answers to the questions he was asking, but was playing games with them.
>
> After two months in the position he held a management retreat to lay the groundwork for how the team would work together. One of the members challenged him on this issue and admitted he found his approach uncomfortable. Andy told him that indeed he did have an assortment of

> solutions to their problems but that his was only one possible answer not the "right" one. He told them that the most important thing for him was to encourage them to find their own solutions and trust their own thinking. He also added how he found it fascinating and full of learning for himself to see the different approaches there were to a single problem or issue.

In organisations where there is a predominance of this mindset there is also a clear preference for independent operational units and local autonomy. Institutional policies and procedures act as guidelines with a degree of flexibility in their application. Interdivisional boundaries are well respected and the belief that 'one size doesn't fit all' supports the use of innovative approaches to meeting customer and market demands.

With a clear value placed on addressing the needs of their customers (clients, constituents), such organisations do their best to ensure that their internal systems and procedures are supportive of the external reality in which they operate. The necessary time is taken to build longer-term sustainable relationship with *all* key stakeholders, and employees are encouraged to share the responsibility for the overall success of the enterprise.

The broader leadership function becomes one of setting clear priorities, negotiating realistic targets and defining clear roles and accountabilities. By creating a customer-centred culture, leadership from this mindset fosters an environment in which individuals feel free to ensure customer satisfaction and express their unique contribution in meeting the organisation's goals.

The process of visioning in these organisations is quite different from those with a strongly compliant mindset. In the latter, the top leader or management team determines the vision and others are asked to buy in. In organisations where self-reliance is valued, each person is encouraged to develop their own personal vision and to engage with others in a process of alignment.

The attitude to change is also markedly different. Rather than a threat to the status quo, change is seen as an opportunity for growth. Conditions are created to ensure that everything is loaded for success. If there is a failure, nobody is hunted down and shot. By taking responsibility for the outcome, those involved seek to learn from their experience.

Until more of us trust ourselves enough to adopt the values and beliefs of this mindset and become willing to shift the status quo, we will continue to see a tendency towards hierarchical thinking patterns. We will remain dependent on structure to define us, rather than seeing that shared purpose and relationships are the primary source of our connectedness. We will also experience increasing levels of stress for as long as we reinforce strong control mechanisms and fail to create the coordinative processes that allow high levels of autonomy in *how* we achieve results.

Needless to say, independence and self-reliance overdone can also have adverse consequences. Individuals who remain vehemently independent find it difficult to create intimate relationships with others, as they equate the notion of sharing with loss of power and an overdependence on others. Organisations too, when overly independent in their orientation, miss opportunities for the co-creative opportunities that come through building alliances.

To trust people enough to be self-determining in the way they choose to achieve the organisation's goals is a huge leap to take for the many leaders locked into a mindset of compliance. In order to thrive in today's changing world, this has to be an essential step in both an individual's and an organisation's continuing growth.

Alliance

As we become increasingly aware of the growing levels of connectivity, our consciousness has to evolve if we are to successfully grapple with the paradox and complexities of global living. Many of us have already discovered that the old ways of thinking no longer address the issues confronting us. The evolution into the leadership orientation that grows out of an *alliance* mindset is the natural next step. It is the least visible and the most necessary as we move more fully into the *Relationship Age*.

The fundamental assumption 'if somebody loses, nobody wins'

underlies this orientation. It provides the platform for the beliefs and behaviours that foster relationships of *interdependence* in a global society. When we operate with this as our primary mindset we are likely to have experiences and insights that shift our perspective to one of interconnection. Having recognised that separation is only a physical phenomenon, we look at life holistically and want to learn more about the spiritual and emotional dimensions.

As we expand our mind to incorporate this perspective we recognise the interrelatedness of everything, and eagerly seek ways to collaborate with others. We add value in ways that help in promoting a world that is sustainable for the generations to come, and fairer to the whole of humanity. We ask the question: '*How do I serve?*'

With a mindset of self-reliance and independence, the emphasis is on autonomy and everyone taking the leadership responsibility for their own lives. In the alliance mindset, relationships shift from independence to interdependence. It is here that we realise the true meaning of authentic leadership power. We see that not only are we responsible for our selves, but we also share in the responsibility for the 'collective'.

We embrace more spiritual values, like compassion and altruism, finding that these bring greater fulfilment and productivity than values that are self-serving and are the hallmark of our ego's survival instinct. This idea of connecting to a higher and more loving purpose is echoed in Wayne Dyer's quote: 'We are not human beings having a spiritual experience, rather we are spiritual beings having a human experience.'

Once we allow ourselves to be guided in this way, we take full responsibility for our thoughts, feelings and actions because we recognise that we are each influencing the way things are in the world. It's an awesome discovery to find that not only are we responsible for the results we get in our own life, but that it is our beliefs and the way we focus them that have a direct impact on the bigger picture every second we're alive.

When we operate from the alliance mindset we suddenly become conscious that we all have access to an infinite source of power – an energy force that encourages us to be more generous and giving of ourselves to others. We find that by holding a higher intention, we open our hearts and minds to alternate points of view, seeing the world through a mosaic of different perspectives and letting go of our attachment to right and wrong. We connect with the deeper knowing of our souls' authority, and unlock our full leadership potential.

From this point of view, leadership is seen as inspirational and is as much about wisdom and *who we are* as it is about knowledge and *what we do*. Those who embrace this perspective let go of much of their need for control and learn to trust their intuition, as well as paying attention to the hard facts. They are able to connect to a bigger purpose that is translatable into concrete action. In the words of Angeles Arrien, 'they have learned to walk the spiritual path with practical feet'.

In working with an alliance mindset, we put self-interest into the background and connect to a higher intention that promotes unity and the sharing of leadership for the good of the whole. This means being open about our strengths and our vulnerabilities, both as individuals and in organisations. We readily share our hopes and fears and the dreams we hold for others and ourselves.

> Some people describe Dave as an enlightened leader because of his ability to engage people in inspiring ways. He is known throughout the company as someone who is in line to 'go all the way to the top'. Dave did not start his working life in business but spent three years, following the completion of his degree, travelling the world. He told me: 'I needed to find out who I was. There were parts of me I liked and others I didn't, there still are, but I wasn't a real person and would simply have followed the rules had I not taken this time.' He described how he had visited and 'worked' in both the richest and the poorest nations and could not help questioning why there was so much inequality.
>
> Now, as he approaches forty, he feels he has both the wisdom and experience to provide leadership in ways that

> are supportive of today's global reality. He says he follows the rules when they make sense in the bigger picture and not when they don't. It is Dave's broader perspective and his willingness to share resources within his organisation in ways that promote greater interdependence that his people find so inspiring. Someone described him like this: 'He is able to wear two hats at the same time. He does what works for his own division at the same time as making sure it works for the whole company. Everyone knows it and that's why we respect him.'

There are still too few organisations operating with a leadership orientation rooted in the alliance mindset. In many institutions there is not yet enough trust and authenticity in relationships to allow the true nature of the human spirit to be safely expressed. However, as with the previous mindset of self-reliance, there are pockets of people (and project teams and divisions within large organisations) that are working hard to foster and develop this leadership orientation.

Organisations that are encouraging its expression are recognisable by the following characteristics. As well as valuing cultural diversity, they seek opportunities for creative synergy and look at personality and style differences as a rich source of potential for growth. Vision is not some fantasy or a dream of an idealised future state, it is the reality against which every choice and decision is made in the present moment. Its function is to shine a light on the road ahead to ensure that each step taken has meaning and direction. In these organisations there are bright enthusiastic people who feel empowered to take responsibility in determining the shape of things to come.

In working with customers these organisations develop relationships with a partnership orientation, seeing the value of the co-creative aspect of such a connection. By partnering, they become an integral part of a strategic alliance in which they work together developing products and services that support the business direction of both parties. This immediately shifts the nature of relationship to one of interdependence, in which each shares the risks and rewards which come from their joint enterprise.

These organisations are proactive and are often seen as the pacesetters or trendsetters in their particular markets or fields. Unlike their compliant cousins, there is a clear orientation to balancing short-term results with strategies of long-term sustainability. Structure is designed to support the strategic direction rather than shape it, and is flexible and facilitative. People are unafraid to make tough decisions, because they know that failure to do so is costly to all.

Roles and accountabilities in relation to a given task, project or process have more meaning than position or status in the hierarchy. People are enthusiastic and excited about their work and no longer see themselves as defined through structure. As a result they invest energy in ensuring high-quality relationships, placing emphasis on building strong internal and external networks.

Some of these organisations believe they share accountability for global stewardship and look at ways to be environmentally conscious (not just legally compliant), as well as socially responsible. They are beginning to accept the challenge laid down by the late Willis Harman, futurist and former president of the Institute of Noetic Sciences. 'Business has become, in the last half of the twentieth century, the most powerful institution on the planet. The dominant institution in any society needs to take responsibility for the whole. This is a new role for business, not yet well understood or accepted.'

Those enterprises that understand this statement actively invest in the development of the leadership capabilities that foster global cooperation. Such organisations realise that the talent needed to be successful in an interdependent world is still in short supply. They recognise that the leadership needed in the twenty-first century is very different from that of the past. They therefore place a premium on creating learning environments that encourage bright people to push the boundaries and challenge their organisation's outdated assumptions. They also put a high value on the people side of the equation and are waking up to the importance of expressing spiritual and emotional intelligence within the context of work.

It is the development of our consciousness, from a predominant mindset of compliance and dependence to an emphasis on alliance and interdependence, that is critical to our transition into a global future. The shift from leadership as a few holding power over the many to leadership as taking personal authorship for our part in the 'whole', is the core of this book.

Reclaiming our Authenticity

As children we needed a clear set of beliefs and rules of behaviour in order to experience belonging and security. But if we never question them and their relevance to our role in this changing world, we are unlikely to adopt the alliance mindset.

There are of course risks and rewards in accepting the challenge of claiming the power of our authentic presence and of leaving the safety of the tried and true. Many people remain unaware of the choices they have to engage in a process of consciousness development, especially where the dominant structures and systems reinforce and reward the compliance mindset.

Friend and educator Lyla Berg describes how people are 'sleepwalking' their way through life, unaware of the power and the potential they have to really make a difference. She speaks of how 'there needs to be a major transformation in the mindset of teachers and the educational system if we are ever to promote the notion of self-leadership and empowerment.'

The shift from seeing ourselves primarily as having an ego-driven personality to seeing ourselves as a soul purposefully experiencing life here on Earth is a challenging but necessary one. There is a growing belief that we are each born with a unique destiny and that through our socialisation process we lose sight of what it is. We are encouraged to turn off our inner light and look outside for the answers to life's questions.

As we learn the rules of compliance the connection with our soul lessens, and we feel a growing sense of separation from our authentic power. The end result is that we become attached to surviving in the material world, acquiring power from position and possessions, rather than developing our deeper spiritual destinies.

Such a strong focus on the physical reality encourages us to remain locked into a mindset of compliance, externalising the voice of authority and making others responsible for the condition of our lives.

In order to share the leadership responsibility in the emerging society we need a clear commitment to looking at who we are 'inside'. We have to rediscover our unique destinies and reclaim our soul's authority, embarking on a journey of authenticity that is as exciting as it is challenging, and as pleasurable as it is painful. The ego does not willingly move out of the driver's seat and accept its role as servant to the soul. In fact, many of the breakthroughs we experience on our way to claiming authentic leadership take us through the shadowy depths of life's experience, as we wrestle with releasing the attachment to our ego identities.

Everyone's passage to this inner source of power is unique as they test new assumptions and challenge existing beliefs. The process of awakening to these different mindsets is not linear, nor is it discrete. All four mindsets have value and we access each as the need arises. The key issue here is whether we are writing our own life's script and consciously choosing to operate predominantly from the mindset that best serves our soul's intention at any given time, or just drifting aimlessly, making others responsible for where we find ourselves in life?

As more of us recognise the existing economic and ecological interdependence, the legitimacy of the leadership style supported solely by a compliance mindset is seriously challenged. The increase in best-selling literature focusing on spiritual meaning and the soul's development suggests that people are already waking up to the need for something very different.

Letting Go

There appear to be at least three major catalysts for making the journey to reconnect to our soul's authority, inspiring us to share leadership responsibility for the state of our world. The first is an increasing level of dissatisfaction with life as it is. The second is disillusionment with the existing orientation to leadership. The third is a deep desire to uncover our unique contribution in the world. Caroline Myss says in *Anatomy of the Spirit*: 'Every human being will encounter a series of challenges that tests their allegiance to heaven. These tests will come in the form of the disintegration of one's physical power base: the inevitable loss of wealth, family, health, or worldly power. The loss will activate a crisis of faith, forcing one to ask, "What is it, or who is it that I have faith in?" or "into whose hands have I commended my spirit?"'

Setting out on the path to reclaim our soul's authority and share leadership in a global society is full of risk and uncertainty. It means freeing ourselves from the ties that bind us to unhealthy yet often comfortable patterns and relationships. It means taking charge of our destiny and becoming accountable for the results of our actions. And it means leaving the comfort of the known, and determining our own soul's code as we search for deeper meaning in our lives. It is a monumental task that can take us into periods of intense questioning and confusion. It can lead us to leave the roles we've been playing for years, in our work and in our close relationships, and to venture into the unknown.

For both individuals and organisations, living authentically requires boldness and a deep commitment to breaking away from the prevailing patterns that maintain the status quo. It means looking at the unconscious beliefs and assumptions that are running our lives, reclaiming our full potential as human beings.

How do we do this? That is what the rest of this book is about. Even the simple awareness that if we want to change the way things are, we have to begin with ourselves is the first step in letting go of the patterns that have shaped us.

3 □

THE SOFT STUFF IS REALLY THE HARD STUFF

The mind divides the world into a million pieces.
The heart makes it whole.
Stephen and Ondrea Levine

EVER SINCE THE SEVENTEENTH century, the scientific paradigm with its emphasis on rational thought has ruled supreme in the West. In a world that valued reason over passion, measurability and replicability became the keys to our development. The less predictable and more emotional matters of the human heart were left, together with the spirit, in the hands of the Church, while our physical body rested somewhere in between!

This age-old 'split' has led us to some remarkable discoveries about the workings of the universe. It has enabled extraordinary technological advances. It has also allowed us to view things through a lens of clear, cool objectivity and to prize a leadership style that values logical thinking and the rational analysis of 'hard' data. Meanwhile, the softer qualities of spirit and imagination have been resting in the shadows. Today, we have reached the limitation of this mindset and its demand for compliance.

There is increasing pressure to reclaim those aspects of the human condition that have been overshadowed. The separation of thought from feeling and of the head from the heart are no longer viable as we recognise the importance to organisational success and personal fulfilment of authentic leadership. In an age when we seek to address the deeper questions of the soul, the drive for wholeness has become the critical issue of any new orientation to leadership.

In addition to the wonderful life-enhancing products that the mechanistic thinking has brought to us, there is also a dark side that has led to the creation of weapons of mass destruction. There are now enough nuclear weapons to destroy every person on the planet twelve times over! In addition, we have the technology to clone ourselves, and if in the pursuit of 'somebody's idea of perfection we deny the subjective reality of the human experience, we are in danger of creating a bizarre future for ourselves.

It is time to face up to some of these challenging moral dilemmas and take the opportunity to confront the fundamental assumptions that have determined the prevailing pattern of Western thought. We all need to open our hearts and expand our minds if we are to embrace a more spiritual orientation to leadership in this emerging global society.

This process of transformation is well underway as we learn to adopt a systems perspective and recognise the patterns of interconnectedness. New disciplines are emerging that integrate the human and the physical sciences. Research into holistic healing is revealing amazing connections between our mind, body, emotions and spirit. Organisations are re-examining their values and structures, embracing a stronger relationship orientation to doing business. Many people in the West are searching for spiritual meaning in their lives, having discovered that the external world doesn't satisfy their deeper inner yearnings.

There is increasing demand for literature in the areas of spiritual philosophy, human consciousness and transpersonal psychology. The formation of stronger community organisations and self-help groups and a growing intolerance for inequity are also indications of the changes taking place. Increasing demand for higher levels of 'transparency' in government and organisations, with traditional religions losing their adherents as people find alternative ways to satisfy their spiritual needs, provide further signals that the old paradigm is giving way to a new one.

As we adopt the leadership orientation supported by the alliance mindest, there is no need to destroy all that has gone before. There is, however, an absolute imperative to actively engage in a process of metamorphosis and expand our current consciousness to include some of the less tangible dimensions of the human experience. It is a time to trust in more than what meets the eye, as we enter into a period of breakthrough change in the way we think and live. Increasing numbers of people from every walk of life are already engaged in this process and see clearly the limitations of the existing leadership orientation. The current economic crises and the stronger focus on sustainable development are highlighting the need for major changes in the way we look at the world.

Healing the Split

It is becoming crystal clear that the split between reason and passion is very costly to each of us, and to the organisations with which we work. The level of stress-related illness has increased significantly and the softer issues of trust, personal purpose, relationship, ethics, innovation and empowerment are the topics of conversations both inside and outside the workplace.

The subjective dimension of life has been undervalued for the last three hundred and fifty years in government, education and business. Many of us are now anxious to reclaim it. We have been standing on one leg long enough and it is no wonder that many individuals and organisations are out of balance.

To reclaim our authentic leadership power and follow the voice of our soul's authority means coming to terms with these softer and less predictable aspects of the human heart. Feelings are a natural part of our experience and understanding their role in our lives is essential to the expansion of consciousness. They influence our moods, our behaviours and our attitudes to life. Without them we would be like the Vulcan Spock or the android Data in *Star Trek*, advanced intellectual beings unable to experience the full spectrum of life here on Earth.

> It was Sunday afternoon when Harry got the call from his boss at head office. Harry was the site manager of a five-hundred-person manufacturing operation. He had worked there since he was in his early twenties and knew every-

one by name. The site was well managed and was a high-quality operation, so the decision to close it came as a complete surprise.

Harry had always been seen as a clear and logical thinker and was not one to express a great deal of emotion. In fact some referred to him as 'hard-headed Harry' because it took so much to arouse any kind of feeling in him! Little could have prepared him for this moment. As he put down the phone his wife told him he turned white. At first he was speechless and then he shared the content of the conversation with her. He had no idea how to go about the process of shutting the plant down. How was he going to tell the people? What about their lives, their families and their futures? He said he felt sick, lost, hopeless all at once and didn't know what to do with his feelings. In the end he decided to shut them away and execute the task not sharing them with anyone.

Fortunately for Harry this didn't last very long. Some of his colleagues at the site told him that his cool clinical approach was causing a lot of anger and alienation, and that he needed to be more open about how he felt with those around him. It was very hard at first because he really didn't know the difference between a thought and a feeling, let alone how to describe it, but with good support both at home and work he was able to get more in touch with his softer side. The site still had to be closed down and the stress was considerable. He went through some very challenging times, confronting feelings he'd always avoided. Upon reflection Harry credited his friends for saving his life. He'd been suffering from a feeling of restriction in his chest and he told them he was sure that had he not expressed how he felt at the time, his heart would have probably 'exploded'!

So why is the soft stuff *really* the 'hard' stuff? First, it's difficult to understand. The language of spirit and emotion is not an integral part of the standard educational system in the West. Until recently only those who had studied the human sciences or who had been through significant emotional and spiritual experiences were likely to be well versed in it. Boys are still told that certain emotions are OK while girls are encouraged to express others.

Second, the soft stuff is 'hard' in the sense of yielding concrete results. We all know that when we are feeling happy, challenged and fulfilled, and are integrating the soft stuff into our day-to-day work, we are more vital and more empowered. We work better when we are respected, listened to and believe we make a difference. The bottom line can only strengthen in environments where the soft stuff flourishes.

With an alliance mindset, thinking and feeling, head and heart, spirit and matter, the words and the music, are complementary not contradictory. It's only fear and the predominance of the dualistic orientation that perpetuates this 'either–or' thinking. If we are to bring it all together, respecting both the soft and the hard stuff, all we need to do is to open our hearts to a more inclusive way of looking at life. In so doing, it is virtually guaranteed that the world will become a very different place and many of the fears, much of the greed and the feelings of mistrust and insecurity would soon disappear.

His Holiness the Dalai Lama says: 'I believe that our underlying or fundamental nature is gentleness, and intelligence is a later development. And I think that if human ability, human intelligence, develops in an unbalanced way, without being properly counterbalanced with compassion, then it can become destructive. It can lead to disaster. . . . When human intelligence and human goodness or affection are used together, all human actions become constructive. When we combine a warm heart with knowledge and education we can learn to respect others' views and others' rights. This becomes the spirit of reconciliation that can be used to overcome aggression and resolve our conflicts.'

So how do we go about reclaiming and integrating both of these critical components of authentic expression into any future orientation to leadership? Let's first take a look at both sides of the same coin.

Thinking Promotes	*Feeling Promotes*
Product Orientation	Relationship Orientation
Task Focus	People Focus
Rational Perspectives	Emotional Perspectives
Emphasis on Analysis	Emphasis on Values
Logical Approaches	Intuitive Approaches
Objectivity	Subjectivity
Separation	Connection
Critique	Appreciation

'The Myers Briggs Type Indicator', originally based on the work of Carl G. Jung, and further developed over the past eighty years by Katharine C. Briggs and Isabel Briggs Myers, identifies an individual's preference strength on each of four dimensions. These are Extroversion and Introversion, Sensing and Intuition, Thinking and Feeling and Judging and Perceiving. Without going into a lot of detail, this instrument is one of the most effective in respecting the value of personality differences we each bring, based on our preference strengths for these dimensions. It also emphasises that we are not thinkers *or* feelers, rather we simply have a preference for one over the other, and that part of our life's journey is to embrace and integrate all of the different aspects.

Another consistent finding in organisations using this instrument at the management level has to do specifically with the Thinking and Feeling dimension. Although the general statistics of the broader population reveal a fifty-fifty split between T and F (and only a bias of 10 per cent based on gender differences), the story inside, at the 'top' of some of the world's major organisations, is very different!

It is not an exaggeration to say that over 90 per cent of those we have tested who hold significant leadership roles in these institutions showed a clear preference for 'Thinking'! In many management teams *no one* had a preference for 'F'. This doesn't mean that feelings and relationships aren't seen as important. What it does mean is that 'Thinking' and an emphasis on task is by far the dominant preference for these managers in making decisions and going about their business. It's simple – *task* and *doing* is more highly valued than *people* and *relating*.

With these kinds of results is it any wonder that there is a need for a stronger relationship orientation? Is it any wonder when you look at the qualities under the Thinking column and those under the Feeling column that we are faced with the leadership dilemmas that are confronting us these days? And is it any wonder that there is a growing crisis of spirit and meaning when those who have been 'running the world' have such a strong preference for objectivity and results? The data are clear; the question is what do we do and how do we each go about owning this heart-centred dimension in providing leadership in the *Relationship Age*?

How many times do we hear leaders say they mustn't get too close to their people? Or that they put on a different persona when they go to work? How often do we hold ourselves back from truly expressing what we feel because we don't think it's appropriate? Yet almost everyone, if asked, will say they want more trust, more openness, more authenticity in their work place, and will look at those around them to go first! It's an age-old conspiracy and one that is becoming more costly to all of us who engage in it.

Energy in Motion

Daniel Goleman, in his grounding book *Emotional Intelligence*, speaks of eight major families of feelings: Anger, Sadness, Fear, Enjoyment, Love, Surprise, Disgust and Shame. He says: 'All emotions are, in essence, impulses to act, the instant plans for handling life that evolution has instilled in us.' So if we deny our feelings and fail to express them, we will block the natural flow of life, and find ourselves unable to claim our full power.

Goleman talks of people having 'two minds, an emotional mind and a rational mind', and that they need to exist in partnership and to work together in 'tight harmony' with one another. It's this marriage between the two that has been sadly missing and has resulted in the leadership of many organisations losing its lustre. Over time, prevailing patterns have taken over and management has become a little mundane, with a loss of inspiration and passion, and an increase in the pressures for compliance.

Feelings are a very real part of our everyday experience, and are rich contributors to the level of openness and authenticity needed for developing healthy relationships. From our soul's perspective they are neither positive nor negative, they simply are what they are – feelings. Some emotions result in heaviness to our energy and others a lightness of being.

Research indicates that when we make the choice to live in ways that lead us to experience peace, happiness and gratitude, the neurochemical reactions influencing the brain and the body promote positive states of health and clarity of mind. If, however, we stay in situations or relationships that cause us to dwell on emotions like fear, anger, guilt, shame, grief or jealousy, for prolonged periods of time, it's a different story. Such conditions create neurochemical responses that promote levels of toxicity in the body upsetting both our physical and mental functioning. Ultimately this can lead to stress-related conditions, physical breakdown and periods of depression.

Intellectually, emotional expression is seen as critical to leadership effectiveness, but when it comes to practice it can be a different story. In working with thousands of people in organisations over the past twenty-five years, I have seen more denial of feelings than their acknowledgement. Often because there is an absence of acceptance and safety for the expression of emotions in the work environment, and also because of a fear of what might happen if feelings are allowed out of the cupboard.

> Graham knew that if he was to go on growing he needed to do some work on himself. His request was straightforward: 'I need help with my feelings!' He had received feedback saying that he was not always mature in his approach, and it left people feeling disrespected. His score on the 'F' dimension was zero, meaning that he had a strong preference for rationalising and analysing when it came to making decisions.

> He didn't suffer fools gladly and his lack of sensitivity was in danger of harming his career. He had an intellectual arrogance that was becoming costly. At first Graham didn't know how to describe his feelings and would confuse them with thoughts – he would 'think' his feelings instead of really feeling them. His fear of what might happen if once he started to really 'feel' was significant. He had some deep-seated resistances that grew out of not wanting to be seen as a 'weak man' and as a result he'd overcompensated.
>
> Fortunately, his commitment to his own growth and his willingness to take some significant personal risks enabled him to open up and integrate the feeling aspect of himself. It took a while and there are still times when he loses sight of the soft stuff and becomes overly hard-headed. However, he is now seen by his boss and his peers to have developed greater leadership competency as a result of his engagement in this process.

In the alliance mindset, feelings are reframed, from being seen as soft and impractical to being powerful sources of productive energy. Emotions are not simply the expression of feelings, but are recognised as E+Motion or 'energy in motion'. By seeing them as a vital well spring of what is needed to energise the most valuable resources of an organisation, the new orientation to leadership places a different value on this aspect of our humanity. The focus then becomes one of removing some of the personal and organisational blocks to their acceptance.

Take a moment to think of the times when you have held back your own expression of feelings in a meeting or in a relationship. Recall how much effort it took and how disconnected from others you felt because of it. It takes enormous energy to keep our feelings in, with significant personal consequences. By learning the skills necessary to express feelings in responsible and respectful ways we become much more authentic and effective. When we learn to do this well within an organisational context, the level of productivity soars and much of the activity that today is wasted in playing the game is used more effectively.

We then feel safe to express our uniqueness, take risks, build close working relationships and appreciate the contribution that each individual makes to the overall results. Organisational environments support personal growth, encourage experimentation and reward behavioural change. The human spirit returns to work and the lights go back on, illuminating the hallways of what were once seen as grey uninspiring institutions. The role of leadership then becomes one of providing a secure and expansive climate for people to bring all of who they are to what they do.

It is often the fear of loss of control, coupled with the judgement that certain emotions are negative, which causes us to hold back our feelings. In doing so, it gives the denied emotion a lot more power. If this is the case, then when it does come to the surface there is much more force behind it and a greater chance that it will take us over. The fear then becomes a self-fulfilling prophecy. What ends up happening is that at some point it will come out in unexpected ways at unexpected times.

> Brian had a very bright future ahead of him. However, he had been growing more and more frustrated with his boss's micro-management, and unfortunately he hadn't learned to express this frustration in ways that were respectful of himself and others. One day he was in a conversation with his boss and completely lost his cool. He admits now that it was unfortunate, but it was too late. His boss was angry at the outburst and had the power to influence his career significantly – which he did. This one single moment cost Brian years of performance excellence. It was a high price to pay for his inability to manage his feelings.

If we don't take control of our emotions they end up controlling us. The key lies in acknowledging the feeling, whatever it is, and then consciously choosing how best to express it and when. It's a skill that can be learned and is essential to accessing the power of the heart in this new orientation to leadership.

Another factor that prevents the expression of emotion is a lack of feeling vocabulary.

Vocabulary of Feelings: Four Major Emotions

Anger	**Sadness**	**Happiness**	**Fear**
Frustrated	*Disappointed*	*Delighted*	*Shameful*
Enraged	*Despairing*	*Joyful*	*Guilty*
Impatient	*Grief-stricken*	*Contented*	*Anxious*
Resentful	*Depressed*	*Blissful*	*Terrified*
Revengeful	*Remorseful*	*Elated*	*Dreading*
Furious	*Distressed*	*Pleased*	*Concerned*
Annoyed	*Miserable*	*Cheerful*	*Worried*
Outraged	*Anguished*	*Ecstatic*	*Alarmed*
Violated	*Heartbroken*	*Lighthearted*	*Scared*

Sometimes we don't always know how to connect words to what we feel and end up thinking or rationalising our feelings instead of voicing them. Certain emotions have always been more acceptable in the working environment than others. On the whole there is still a strong expectation that feelings should be handled at home and in the social milieu, and not brought to the office. So we end up taking our minds and our bodies to work, leaving our hearts and spirits at home.

Once we reconnect to our soul's authority, expand our thinking and include the potential contribution of our emotional experience, we can provide the heartfelt leadership that supports the expression of this rich source of human energy.

The Business of Spirit

It's as silent as the air we breathe, invisible to the eye, intangible, immeasurable; and yet when it's present, we know it. It's the creative thought, the inspired speech, the enthusiastic contribution, and the essence of connection in relationships. One definition of 'Spirit' in

Collins' English Dictionary is 'the force or principle that animates the body of living things'. In other words it's energy, it's the inner light, our very life force. Without spirit we cease to be fully alive.

In our Western religious framework, spirit has been separated from matter and thought more often than not. Until recently it had not been considered a critical element in achieving high levels of performance effectiveness. Happily, spirit is making a comeback today as we recognise the importance of spiritual values in providing leadership, building teams, acknowledging connectedness and achieving results. Management is beginning to see that spirit really matters!

Peter Russell, author of *Waking up in Time* and *From Science to God*, talks about a Spiritual Renaissance: 'We must find again the wisdom that originally shone through the great religions, the wisdom that illuminated the minds of great saints and sages. And we need to put this perennial philosophy of human consciousness in the language of our times, in the expressions and forms appropriate to . . . the third millennium.'

Such a process of rediscovery means that if we are to provide authentic leadership in this new era of relationships, we must work from the inside out and look first at the relationship we have with our spiritual Self. We need to reconnect to the wellspring of our own wisdom and the power of our soul's knowing. There has never been a better time to rediscover how to trust and believe in all the parts of ourselves and become whole again.

However, in a society that has been culturally hypnotised to look outwards and to forget and even to fear the inner riches of the spirit, it is a tough challenge. The voice of our spirit is so often drowned out by all the noise of our doingness that we lose sight of our true path and end up unfulfilled.

It happens to almost all of us at some time because we are encouraged to be outer-focused, educated with a strong bias towards action. This leaves little or no time for inner journeying in the form of meditation and reflection. So we become human doings and human havings, and our being-ness gets forgotten, except perhaps at weekends and on holiday. Even then, I wonder how many of us really stop long enough to listen to the voices of our souls.

The price of our outer-directed action orientation is seen on an individual level in lower levels of self-esteem, more unhappiness in relationships, widespread patterns of addiction and in the increase of chronic illnesses like colitis, arthritis, migraines, high blood pressure, burnout, heart disease and obesity, to name a few. When we don't take the time to regenerate and reconnect to our inner source of vitality then there's a high probability that our energy will be blocked on the physical, mental and emotional levels. This gets manifested as stress-related problems as we lose touch with the source of our inspiration. In organisations, if management inhibits the expression of spirit there will be low energy, apathy, cynicism, mistrust, risk-aversion, power games, higher levels of absenteeism, sabotage and lowered productivity.

For as long as we maintain a leadership orientation that supports the myth of separation, of inner from outer, we will continue to lose energy. When we recognise the reality of holism, connection and relatedness we can unblock these restrictions. Michael Ray says in *New Traditions in Business*: 'The new paradigm is more than just a move to the powers of technology or the individual mind. It is a move toward the spirit; to inner qualities such as intuition, will, joy, strength and compassion. Spirituality in the new paradigm does not refer to religion but rather to the power of wisdom and authority and the connection and wholeness of humanity.'

The Tao, the Koran, the Kabala and the Bible all speak to this notion of unity, as well as sharing other spiritual values including compassion, truth, forgiveness, love, humility and service. When examining the core values of major corporations like 3M, Microsoft, GE, Hewlett Packard, Motorola, Pfizer, AT&T, Coca-Cola, Nike and Walt Disney, you only have to scratch the surface to find them. The question at issue here is: 'How do we develop leadership behaviours to encourage the expression of these spiritual values in ways that are truly supportive of the emerging global society?'

If we take a close look at the world as it is today, the core purpose of any new orientation to leadership has to be to shine a light on these values so that they come alive in our everyday experience. We need to inspire a new kind of leadership consciousness that reclaims the soft stuff and reignites our authentic power. In order to do this we must rediscover our faith in the innate goodness of the human spirit and let go of the many fears that cause us to hold back the full expression of our co-creative potential.

4 □

POWER AND THE 'F' WORD

Fear is a wonderful servant but a lousy master
Max Magee

IT'S A FOUR-LETTER WORD beginning with 'F', it holds us back from some of the richest rewards of the human experience and it is singularly the highest invisible cost on the balance sheet of most organisations. *Fear* is the biggest consumer of human energy and drains our authentic power.

It saps our strength, wrecks our self-esteem, is a huge barrier in creating healthy relationships and prevents us from taking the necessary risks that will bring peace and fulfilment. In its extreme, it drives people to harm themselves and destroy others. In looking around at today's current reality, fear is so clearly the trigger for many of the world's ills and the single biggest issue behind poor performance at work.

Understanding fear and the role it plays in our lives is a critical issue in reclaiming our soul's authority and sharing accountability for global leadership. Allowing it to remain an unconscious driver keeps us locked in unhealthy patterns of dependency which take us away from the alliance mindset.

Any form of leadership that has a fear-based orientation is ultimately self-defeating. The very nature of fear causes restriction and contraction on every level of the human experience. It may result in quick action in an emergency but over prolonged periods it is extremely destructive, both individually and collectively. If we are to take leadership, and make our contribution to the world, we must 'name' our fears and face them.

When we do this we can move forward and free the hold fear has over us. Until we do it will stop us from fully expressing our true potential. Uri Geller says in *Mind Medicine*: 'We cling to fear even though it repels us, as though ignoring such a power is tempting fate. Therefore letting go of fear is frightening. Dealing with fear means facing up to it and challenging it.'

One of the major drivers to creating the fear-based society that reinforces the compliance and defiance mindsets is the very principle on which the West has been educated – survival of the fittest. This single principle has led to the development of some of the most pervasive beliefs about life, such as 'there's not enough to go around', 'it's a dog eat dog world', 'win as much as you can', and 'the more you have the bigger you are'. In other words, resources are scarce and you have to get what you can, and hold on to it, or you'll be left hungry and needy.

The leadership behaviours these beliefs reinforce often stem from deep feelings of insecurity. Not only do they encourage territorialism and unnecessary competition, they also cause people to acquire more than they will ever need and then become reluctant to share it with those who have less. So the rich get richer and the poor get poorer, as the principle of survival of the fittest gets reinforced.

It is through perpetuating the notion of scarcity and allowing ourselves to be driven by a consumer mentality that we are likely to create the situation we fear most. The prognosis for our survival is not good if we continue to think and behave in these ways.

The beliefs that lead to these behaviours usually operate behind our conscious awareness and hold us back from the inward journey to our soul's source. They are at the root of our biggest fears, influencing the ways we live, the choices we make and how we manage our organisations. The fears these assumptions generate are complex and deeply rooted in our psyches.

Below are descriptions of three of the most popular ones. If we are to take authentic leadership we have to face them in ourselves and in others. Once we understand fear and the role it plays, then it can no longer threaten us. We can then free the dark power fear holds over us. Once we make the commitment to live from what Gary Zukav calls 'the seat of the soul', we begin the process of releasing fear from our lives. From this place we are able to create an orientation to leadership built on relationships of interdependence.

Fear of Failure

This is one of the most widespread fears that runs our lives, creating high levels of personal stress and costing companies untold millions of dollars every year in lost performance. It's an interesting one because it can drive us to very different behaviours. In some of us, it promotes dependency and an absence of self-responsibility, causing us to play it safe. In doing so, we are afraid to make changes and we strive to keep things just the way they are. We do things the way we've always done them, not wanting to screw it up by trying something new.

This fear causes us to stay away from taking risks and to resent those who may be asking us to make adjustments either in our work or in our personal lives. The resistance to change that is generated by this fear keeps people and organisations stuck in old behaviours, reinforcing traditional leadership styles and shutting out inspiration. In other words, a top-down style that encourages caution and long, slow, careful decision-making processes which minimise disruption to the status quo!

> Mike was known as a solid performer. He had been put in his position to look for new product and marketing opportunities. His boss was renowned for being hard and liked to control the whole show. At first Mike was enthusiastic and thought that he could still work creatively within the situation. However, it wasn't long before his deep-seated fear of failure caused him to succumb to the pressure from up above, and as a result he became more and more careful. He didn't want to screw up and in the end was afraid to take risks in case they didn't work. He began adopting the behaviours of his boss and despite feeling lousy about

himself, he chose to remain in the position. Over time his fear of failure led to a lack of action and an absence of positive change. Mike became stressed and his health began to suffer; so too did his career.

Others, who have a deep fear of failure, become the over-achievers of the world. They are often found in significant leadership roles. Driven by the need to overcome the fear of failing, such folks work long and hard in reaction to this usually unconscious motivator. If they don't become aware of this underlying driver, they experience a hollow quality to their success, never really feeling worthy of what they have achieved. These people, unlike those described above, frequently seek out risks to prove to themselves that they're unafraid to fail.

When we operate with this motivation, we tend to test ourselves, sometimes to extraordinary lengths, in an attempt to overcome this fear. As with other fears, until we acknowledge it, make peace with it and withdraw the energy we have invested in it, it will continue to hold power over us.

Awareness of what lies behind our behaviour patterns is the first step to removing the power that a fear has in our lives. Because we are often blind to it, we sometimes need someone else to shed light on this part of our lives. Asking the following questions can help:

- Am I setting my own criteria for success?
- Do I feel someone somewhere is judging me – if so, who?
- What would I do if I knew I couldn't fail?
- What is the risk of changing? What is the risk of not changing?
- Why am I working so hard?

Fear of Loss of Control

As change speeds up and the future grows even more unpredictable, fear of loss of control is finding many a fertile field for getting a foothold! Those of us who have this fear as a companion find ourselves writing pages of to do lists and never quite having enough time to complete them. It doesn't matter how hard or how long we work, there's always more; and the feeling of dissatisfaction with not having things under control drives us ever more deeply into this fear. In fact, the more this fear takes hold the more desperately we try to control everyone and everything, fearing that if we don't something will fall between the cracks and won't be done right!

> Sarah had always achieved good results in leading her team to new standards of performance. She was highly thought of and although she was seen as a little bit of a 'control freak', the people who worked with her found it acceptable. In her late thirties she decided to create her own company. She had both the experience and the resources. However, with the added responsibility of the enterprise now being hers, her need to control everything and everyone became much more intense.
>
> Her fear of loss of control led to extremely long working hours and a lot of dissatisfaction with her employees. It was a really tough situation because when she let go and allowed others to take responsibility they never 'got it right'. It was a catch-22 – she was stressed either way. Today, her inability to get to the root of this fear is having a significant impact on her health and her family life, and she feels there is no way out. Sarah is working six days a week and on the seventh worries about what she hasn't got done and has yet to do.

Perfectionism is often hiding in the shadows of those who fall under the influence of this fear. Until they see that this is an insatiable desire, they are likely to be driven, and to drive others, to extreme levels of stress as they strive to achieve perfection in all that they do and all that they are.

Intimate relationships can be very challenging for these people because intimacy means feelings, and feelings by their very nature are unpredictable. So in our personal lives the fear of loss of control can hold us back from building authentic relationships and allowing others to get close to us. If we are unwilling to take the risks that lead to change, and are afraid of leaving our comfort zones, we may spend years in patterns of over-controlling our partners, our children, our jobs and our whole environment. Unable to trust our own inner knowing, we feel a loss of joie de vivre, and the gradual suppression of our life force.

Fear of loss of control keeps many organisations mired in patterns of dependence and compliance. Institutions where this fear runs rampant hold on to a paternalistic leadership orientation with resistance to change driving much of the decision-making.

What is missing in these often highly structured climates is the willingness on the part of those in leadership roles to trust people enough to get things done in ways that are different from the past. As a consequence, such organisations are populated by what some refer to as 'control junkies' who manage minutiae in order to prevent any possible hint of chaos and confusion that might arise from a bout of creativity.

The tougher the operating climate, and the more the belief in scarcity takes root, the more the fear of loss of control takes hold. Instead of looking for ways to create new opportunities, a cold wet blanket descends from on high, dampening everyone's spirit and focusing people's energy on cutting costs and achieving short-term results. The consequences of such a one-dimensional focus are huge losses of inspiration, and the simple goodwill of the people. Those with high potential begin to look elsewhere and the organisation finds itself stuck in a fear-based orientation from which it is hard to break free.

Asking the following questions can help:

- What would happen if I let go of control?
- What personal price do I pay for my drive for perfection?
- Do I really have things under control or is it an illusion?
- How does my fear of 'loss of control' control me?

Fear of Rejection

This is the third of the fears that often prevent us from expanding our minds, owning our authentic leadership power and embracing the alliance mindset. Like the previous ones, it holds us back from building really healthy relationships of mutual trust and respect. However, it plays itself out in more subtle ways than the previous two, because it operates on a deeper emotional level.

When we are young we know instinctively that our survival depends upon not being rejected, so many of us behave in ways that will gain approval and therefore belonging. As we get older, if this fear is central, we find ourselves telling lies and denying our authentic voice in order to be accepted. This happens a lot in close relationships and encourages patterns of co-dependence that prevent us from being open to deeper levels of intimacy. The growth potential of many marriages and other forms of partnership are blocked by the assumption that the other can, and will, reject us.

Much of this fear arises from our earliest experiences of being rejected by our parents, our siblings, our peers or other authority figures in our lives. The depth of the fear depends on the intensity of these early rejections, and how we coped with them. For example, if someone constantly had their thoughts and ideas rejected, they may find it difficult to believe that their point of view has value; and therefore may be unable to assert themselves. If, however, someone felt rejected for being who they are as 'a person', they may *never* again show up in their true colours.

> Stephen was the middle child and was very different from his elder brother. He was just under one year old when his little sister was born. He remembers how his father took time to play with his big brother and how his mother took care of his sister. He said that sometimes he felt completely unseen – almost as if he was invisible. 'As I grew up my brother spent more time with me but I carried the feeling of having been rejected at such an early age very deeply.' He admitted that it affected every part of his life, from his attitude at school to his choice of career. He found it hard

to trust anyone in case they got too close and then rejected him.

Stephen married in his mid-twenties but his wife left him within three years. He then avoided any further intimate relationships until his late thirties. After the death of both parents, he made the choice to face his fear. He was in his mid-forties before he at last made peace with it. Today, he admits that the shadow is still there but it doesn't influence his life choices in the same way.

Depending on the nature of our first experiences of rejection and the depths of the wounds they created, we will behave in different ways as adults. Compliance, or working in ways to avoid the disapproval of others, is one way to avoid further rejection, but it also prevents us from coming to terms with this issue. Alternatively, we can engage in behaviours in which we set ourselves up for rejection so that we can perpetuate our belief that we are not good enough. It's one way of maintaining dependence and co-dependence and avoiding claiming full responsibility for our lives.

Another way that this fear can affect us is by leading us to constantly reject ourselves. We develop an inner critic that criticises us, causing feelings of deep self-rejection about our competence, and our self-worth. Rejecting ourselves first serves as a preemptive strike with subsequent rejections from others simply confirming our own inner belief. Alternatively, or sometimes in addition, we develop a strong streak of judgement, leading us to judge others and behave in ways that are arrogant and dismissive. All forms of rejection emanate from a lack of love and deep respect for who we are.

The behaviour patterns of rejection are very much alive in every organisation, though they may vary in their intensity. Terms like 'they shoot the messenger around here', 'tell them what they want to hear', and 'we're a "good news" company', are indicators of the presence of this fear. The consequences are far-reaching. People become afraid of telling the truth as it really is, reinforcing a cultural norm of political politeness. The result is that the further up the hierarchy you are, the less likely you are to hear the truth. The collusion is enormous, and people then question why the leadership of the organisation is out of touch with what's really going on!

It is difficult to build an environment of openness and trust if fear of rejection is widespread in an organisation. Both management and employees need to look at how they perpetuate the fear of rejection and what they need to do to change it if they are ever to create a climate of genuine empowerment.

Asking the following questions can help:

- What was my first experience of being rejected?
- How does it affect my behaviour today?
- How do I reject myself?
- What and how do I reject others?
- How does the fear of rejection control my life choices?

Shining a Light on the Shadow

Fear by its very nature is instinctive and designed to protect us; it can ensure our physical survival when we are threatened. Colleague Paul Sullivan said in a recent conversation: 'Fear is not all bad, it can create a sense of caution warning us of potential danger and creating safety – which we all need under certain circumstances. What we don't need is the fear that holds us back, the fear that is limiting, debilitating and destructive – the fear that stops us from living.'

The problem arises when we allow fear to take on the role of the master rather than servant in our lives. When our ego is dominant, fear will run our lives, sometimes in obvious ways and other times with more subtlety. Once our souls take over, fear has little real influence other than to warn us when our physical world is threatened.

It is our ego-driven personalities that can hold us back from the inner journey to our soul's authority, making us afraid of what we might find if we stopped and took a look inside. Instead we often stay in jobs and relationships that are not satisfying, fearing the unknown and afraid of the pain and adjustment that a change would bring. We hold ourselves back from new adventures unaware of the opportunities available to us. In so doing we fail to claim the leadership power we have to create a life of fulfilment, justifying our absence of action by telling ourselves that we are unworthy of this or it's just 'the way it is'.

Nelson Mandela, in his inaugural speech as South African President, quoted Marianne Williamson: 'Our deepest fear is not that we are inadequate; our deepest fear is that we are powerful beyond measure; it is our light not our darkness that frightens us . . . As we are liberated from our fear, our presence automatically liberates others.'

Many of us have been educated to believe that power of any kind corrupts; that it is manipulative and negative. We have all experienced plenty of examples to reinforce those beliefs. But our inner power is naturally loving and supportive unless it is distorted by fear. In fact, Caroline Myss describes love as 'the only authentic power'.

If we are to fully embrace our authentic presence and continue to expand our leadership potential we need to become aware of any fears that hold us back. We have to make peace with our 'shadow', those unconscious aspects of our personality that keep us in the dark. These are parts of ourselves that we most often project onto others and that remain disowned in ourselves.

The shadow part of us is like the basement, or loft, of a house into which we have pushed our fears and our unfulfilled desires. It is the part of our personality that we don't want to accept, including the wishes and dreams in which we have lost faith. The shadow is often thought of as dark and dusty, it is where we have been burying stuff for years.

The more we have denied, the bigger the task of sorting it out becomes, and the more reluctant we are to face it. After a while the shadow stuff begins to affect the rest of the house and the effort to keep it all hidden consumes more and more of our total energy. The result is that some people feel tired and irritable, less alive and more highly stressed; others engage in addictive habits like too much drinking, smoking and eating, or working too hard. Many of us will go to great lengths to distract ourselves from having to turn inward and face the shadow.

Once we become aware of these behaviours, either through feedback from others or from our own increasing levels of dissatisfaction and the varying crises in our life, we have a choice. We can either continue as we are, using more and more of our energy to keep it all in, or we can face the shadow. We can reacquaint ourselves with those aspects of our personality that we have put to one side, and reclaim the power that is held back in fear.

The term 'mid-life crisis' has been popularly associated with shining light on the shadow side of our personalities, but we don't have to wait until then. We can choose to look at both our hopes and our fears and reconnect to our soul's deeper knowing at any time. Sometimes we can do this by attending seminars and workshops, or by working with skilled professionals who can help us to understand and make peace with ourselves. Alternatively, simply reading, meditating and keeping a journal can engage us in this process of soul-discovery.

This exploration of the shadow is often described as a key part of our spiritual journey, a passage in which we face our dark side and our inner demons and claim our light. It requires courage and support because it is often a time of considerable pain and confusion. But the riches and the gifts are beyond measure.

Everyone's shadow is unique. So too is their journey into it, yet for many of us there are common themes. It tends to hold our shame and our guilt, our anger and our sorrow, our insecurity and despair and our absence of self-worth. It houses all our resentments and regrets, as well as the judgements that have been made about us, and the ones we have made about others. It holds our vulnerability and our buried secrets; and it is the doorway to our deepest desires for love, peace and freedom.

By facing this part of our self and working to release the fear associated with these shadowy depths, we free up a new source of energy. We reclaim our inner authority and discover more of the compassionate, forgiving and loving parts of ourselves. We experience a sense of humility and awe at the wonders of the universe and we find ourselves more respectful of others' differences.

In doing this work, we rediscover our co-creative potential and increase our levels of authenticity. We become more willing to take leadership and contribute to other people's lives. We are more trusting of our intuition and more trusting of our abilities to make the right choices. Our relationships become more honest as we open to deeper levels of intimacy. We no longer need to stay distanced from others, afraid that they may see us for who we really are – we've done the work, we know ourselves, and we have nothing to hide. Shining the light into the shadow frees up the power held in the darkness, a power that, without our 'fear of fear' to distort it, is generous in its desire to be of service and support to others.

The Organisational Shadow

In the leadership of large institutions such power is transformative and can release untold levels of productivity that lie dormant in the shadows of many traditional organisations. However, turning the lights back on requires an extraordinary commitment, given the years of reinforcement of the compliant mindset. Many of those in corporate and governmental management roles have become 'culturally comatosed', unaware of the behaviour patterns that cause so much of people's potential to be shut away.

With a shortage in the leadership competencies needed for today's reality and an increase in what the McKinsey Company calls the 'War for Talent', many managers are beginning to wake up to the fact that something needs to change. Young high-potentials with big dreams are not willing to wear the corporate straitjacket of conformity and the mask of approval. They are unwilling to put their souls to sleep and their ambition on the back burner, in order to 'play the game'. The cost is too high for these people to stay in such organisations, so they become easy prey for hungry headhunters. Companies are losing their brightest people and need to clear away the 'stuff' that casts a shadow if they are to attract and retain the bright lights of the future.

With growing evidence that it is the beliefs and behaviours comprising the alliance mindset that are needed to be successful in a global society, most organisations have a lot of 'inner' work to do. In a world increasingly characterised by networks, mergers, acquisitions, stronger relationships with customers and global economic interdependency, institutions have to come to terms with the fears that promote a leadership style based on tight controls and that prevent people from building authentic relationships with each other.

Pressures are increasing for paternalistic organisations to face their shadow sides and free up the powerful energy that is being held back by outdated patterns of behaviour – patterns of behaviour that have caused people to shut away their creative spirits, leave their emotions at home, compete internally, protect scarce resources and fear the consequences of not pleasing the boss.

At the personal level, pressure is also increasing on many of us to face our fears, as high levels of stress and anxiety become the major triggers to burnout and chronic illness. One of the first things we can do is to let go of expecting others to change in the hopes they will make our lives more comfortable, relieving us of the necessity to do this work. Secondly, we need to take long hard looks at the payoff we get for remaining attached to our fears. We need to identify what we might have to give up if we are to free all the energy consumed by the myriad of insecurities that prevent us from claiming leadership. It is only when we discover that fear is our teacher, and not our enemy that we can accept the full riches of our authentic power.

LIVING WITH ENERGY

Trust in the Force, may the Force be always with you.
Obe Wan Kanobe

FOR CENTURIES, PHILOSOPHERS, MYSTICS and healers have believed in the presence of a field of energy surrounding the human body that is reflective of our overall well-being. Many of the ancient spiritual and healing traditions refer to the existence of a series of energy 'centres' that, when operating in harmony, promote health on all the four levels of existence – mental, emotional, physical and spiritual.

Knowledge about these 'centres' was kept secret, and passed down by word of mouth from teacher to pupil, as part of the wisdom traditions, but references to such subtle energies associated with the soul's experience have been around for a long time, and can be found in the esoteric teachings of the major world religions.

The rebalancing of energy is also at the core of many of the complementary healing approaches, such as acupuncture, reiki, shiatsu, homeopathy, aromatherapy, Ayurveda, colour therapy and others. The belief that physical, emotional and mental disease result from an imbalance in our energy field informs much of the practice of these healing professions. In addition, an understanding of the human energy system is a key part of the practice of yoga, meditation, Qui gong, t'ai chi and most of the martial arts.

In recent years more awareness of this 'subtle energy field' has been brought into the mainstream of Western thought to promote greater integration and consciousness about its relevance to our day to day life. One of the most prominent and insightful works to date is Caroline Myss' *Anatomy of the Spirit: The Seven Stages of Power and Healing.*

Her work is a masterpiece and promotes Western understanding of the relationship of this energy body to our health and our sense of personal responsibility. She describes it in her book: 'Your physical body is surrounded by an energy field that extends as far out as your outstretched arms and the full length of your body. It is both an information centre and a highly sensitive perceptual system. We are constantly 'in communication' with everything around us through this system, which is a kind of conscious electricity that transmits and receives messages to and from other people's bodies.'

Today, as the language of energy and emotions becomes more prominent in public and organisational arenas, it is important to take this one step further and include an understanding of the concept of human energy in the context of the changing nature of leadership. Such understanding is vital to becoming aware of the right use of power in a global society.

The Chakras

The 'chakras', are seven major energy centres that sit in alignment with the spine. They are often described as 'wheels of light', because each chakra spins and emits a colour. (Chakra is a Sanskrit word for wheel.) Some people are able to see a light surrounding the human body, usually called the aura, and can distinguish the position and radiance of each of the chakras.

After many hundreds of years of study by very diverse populations, there is a good deal of agreement about their location and function. The first three are located below the breastbone and are referred to as the lower chakras. These tend to be concerned more with physical and emotional energy. The fourth chakra, located in the region of the heart, acts as the bridge to the three higher chakras, which are associated with the mental and spiritual dimensions. (See Table 2.)

The seven major chakras are also related to the endocrine system and the functioning of organs that are close to their location. For example, the 'heart chakra' influences the heart and the lungs, the 'solar plexus chakra' influences the adrenal glands and the kidneys,

THE SEVEN KEYS

Honouring the Mystery

Trusting Intuition

Voicing Truth

Inspiring Love

Sharing Power

Generating Passion

Establishing Security

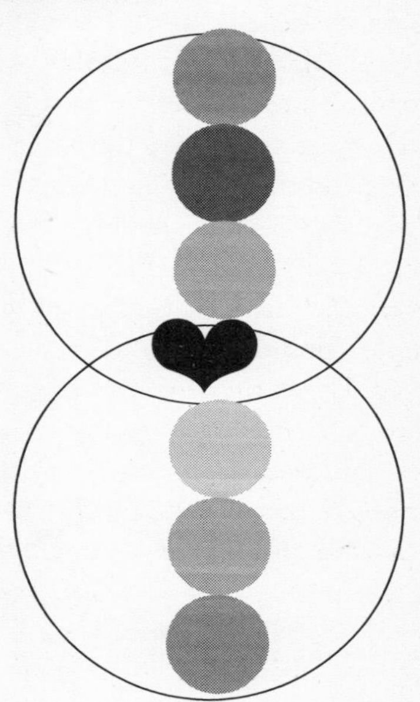

LEADERSHIP KEY	NAME OF CHAKRA	COLOUR	LOCATION	FUNCTION	FOCUS OF DEVELOPMENT*
1. ESTABLISHING SECURITY	First Root Chakra *Muladhara*	Red	Base of Spine	Stablility Belonging	Self-Awareness
2. GENERATING PASSION	Second Sacral Chakra *Svadhisthana*	Orange	3–4 cm below the navel	Partnerships Sexuality	Self-Worth
3. SHARING POWER	Third Solar Chakra *Manipura*	Yellow	Solar Plexus	Power Will Responsibility	Self-Esteem
4. INSPIRING LOVE	Fourth Heart Chakra *Anahata*	Green Rose Pink	Centre of Chest	Love Compassion	Self-Love
5. VOICING TRUTH	Fifth Throat Chakra *Visuddha*	Turquoise Blue	Throat	Communication Personal Authority	Self-Expression
6.TRUSTING INTUITION	Sixth Brow Chakra (Third Eye) *Ajna*	Indigo Blue	Centre Brow	Higher Knowing Wisdom	Self-Knowledge
7. HONOURING THE MYSTERY	Seventh Crown Chakra *Sahasrara*	Violet or Gold	Top of Head	Unity Transcendence Divine Will	Self-Realisation

*Used with permission from the work of Manuela Terraluna

and so on. In the more established healing traditions, disease and illness are seen to result from energy imbalances in a given energy centre or in the energy body as a whole. Professionals in the area of complementary medicine are able to work with individuals to rebalance the energy, thus helping to restore the person to full health, frequently without the need of either surgery or drugs.

Understanding the chakras and their functioning is an important step in reclaiming our authentic leadership power. With this knowledge we gain significant insight into the relationship we have with ourselves, with others and with the world around us. We also begin to get a clearer picture of why our life is energetically 'the way it is' and accept the responsibility to make the needed changes. Becoming more familiar with this system can help us free up any of our life force that is held in emotional wounds and patterns of behaviour that produce irregular levels of energy and stress-related disorders.

When we are feeling good about ourselves and have the sense that we're firing on all cylinders, it is likely that the energy is flowing freely through the chakras, from the top of our heads through to the soles of our feet. When we are out of sorts and our energy is low for extended periods, it is most likely that we have some work to do with one or more of the chakras. Both acute and recurring symptoms in a certain part of the body give us a clue as to which chakra needs attention. Burnout, chronic fatigue and other energy-related disorders are all indications that we are not effectively managing the overall flow of these subtle forces.

The role of the chakras goes way beyond the physical realms of existence. They provide the keys to accessing authentic leadership and gaining clarity about our soul's intention. In looking at the leadership challenges facing us today we clearly have to become more knowledgeable about how we use and abuse human energy, both personally and collectively. Many of us are just becoming aware of the impact of these subtle forces on our relationships and our lives.

Our energy, and how we focus it, is at the core of this new orientation to leadership. Recognising and connecting to the source of our authentic power and understanding how we gain energy and how we lose it are as crucial to our effectiveness as they are to our health and spiritual well-being. If we are to take personal authorship of our lives and share the accountability for shaping leadership in a global reality, then it becomes essential to deepen our personal awareness of these sources of energy and the true impact of these powerful forces.

The Seven Keys

We know we are at a critical turning point in our history. We know that we cannot continue as we have done in the past and expect to have a sustainable future. We all know that a significant transformation in the way we think and behave is needed, and even though we may want to deny this necessity, it becomes more obvious with each moment.

A quotation from Vaclav Havel provides a clear perspective of the choice we face. 'Without a global revolution in the sphere of human consciousness, nothing will change for the better in the sphere of our being as humans, and the catastrophe toward which this world is headed – be it ecological, social, demographic or a general breakdown of civilisation – will be unavoidable.'

Any leadership that is to be effective in the face of such a transformation has to be sourced from an inner orientation to power and deeply rooted in spiritual values. If it is not, then corruption and devastation are inevitable. Unlocking the energy of *The Seven Keys* takes us on an inner journey of soul-discovery and provides a framework for working with human energy in transformative ways. These are the Keys for accessing the full potency of our leadership and providing the inspiration needed for such a revolution. They are designed to unlock the potential we each have for being fully alive in the moment and for creating a world that is less destructive and more acknowledging of the human spirit.

Each Key accesses a vital force essential to claiming our authentic leadership power. As we embrace the alliance mindset we find ourselves driven not by the need to achieve but rather by a desire to contribute. In reconnecting to our soul's authority we are guided to where we access higher states of awareness that promote increased global cooperation and deeper personal fulfilment. The Keys enable us to open the doors and free the energies trapped in the past and the future and reclaim our true potential as co-creators of our global reality.

In the following seven chapters, the Keys are described in terms of both a process (e.g. establishing) and a result (e.g. security). Their function and qualities are explored in some depth on both an individual and a broader level. Understanding the nature of the Keys is only the first step. If we are to walk through what Naomi Ozaniec refers to as the 'Seven Gateways' in ways that are of real value, there are certain fears we have to face and spiritual values we need to embrace.

Although this framework is presented in a linear manner the development of the Keys and the evolution of consciousness is not. The chakras form a unified field of energy. Each one is an essential element to the functioning of the whole. Sometimes the energy flows freely through these vortices, while other times it is restricted. For each one of us, the journey to reclaim our authentic power and our soul's authority will be different, with some common threads.

The description of the Seven Keys provides a platform for understanding this journey and the nature of leadership needed in this age of relationships. They open the doors to our inner worlds and to greater levels of authenticity and vitality. By turning our attention inward we expand our capacity for experiencing life in ways that keep our feet firmly planted on the ground, while reconnecting to higher dimensions of spiritual energy.

Part Two

THE SEVEN KEYS

ESTABLISHING SECURITY

We crave not just real estate but relationships.
Rob Parsons

THE FIRST KEY

Characteristics
Unlocked
Secure, feet on the ground, anchored, stable, participative, physically alert, contributive, sense of belonging, connected
Locked
Insecure, stubborn, inflexible, resistant to change, stuck, ungrounded, flighty, isolated, lacking identity, exclusionary

Personal Implications

THE ENERGY OF THE First Key supports us in building a strong foundation that is unshakeable even in a turbulent world. Our authentic leadership power comes from an experience of deep inner security and a feeling of being at home within ourselves. It grows out of our ability to connect with the voice of our soul's authority and to feel 'safe' wherever we are and whomever we're with. We can look at security through two lenses – physical security and emotional security. This Key connects us with both and has to do with being at ease in the material world.

Most of our early socialisation encourages us to look for a sense of security outside ourselves. When we're young we need to feel secure in a home and in relationships with our family and friends. In Maslow's hierarchy of needs this is the basic need that has to be met to allow us to grow. We need to feel a level of personal safety in order to experience physical and emotional well-being and to build a solid foundation for life's journey.

When we focus our attention on this Key, we learn about our *relationship to groups of others*. We take the first steps to developing self-awareness of the impact of our behaviour on others and theirs on us. Part of our nature at this level of existence is the need to feel a sense of belonging, whether of a family, a team, an organisation or a culture. It is important as human beings to be a part of 'a collective.' Through this we experience being bonded to others and have the physical security we need to survive. Without roots it is hard to grow and to reach our full potential. We all need to feel a sense of connection to others otherwise we will find it hard to experience many of the pleasures of being human.

As we grow up it is important to begin to look for the sense of security within ourselves and to let go of the need for others to provide it. We will still need friends and family to help us, creating safe spaces in which we can learn to establish a deeper sense of our inner security. However, if we become overly dependent on other people or things outside ourselves to feel secure, we begin the slow process of eroding our authentic power.

Each collective (family, team, organisation, etc.) has its own set of beliefs and assumptions, and by adopting these we get membership and identity. We share a common ideology, or 'common sense', and as a result become accepted into the group. All of us know the experience of being part of a family or a workgroup and the quirks, jokes, rituals and rules that make it unique. It gives us a sense of physical safety and emotional acceptance. It can also be a trap if we allow the *fear of abandonment* to take over and simply allow the collective to determine our path, never taking leadership of our own lives.

Freedom and Security

Sometimes we find ourselves so entrenched in situations that we can't move forward. Afraid of disapproval, we stay put, even though we know it is draining our energy. What was once secure becomes claustrophobic, and we are left feeling locked in and resentful. This First Key has to do with feeling secure with others and within ourselves, so that we are equally at ease being 'a part of', and also 'apart from,' the group.

If we have too much of our focus here it is hard to claim our soul's authority and to establish our identity separate from the group or family unit. Sometimes we have to break free from long-standing relationships in our personal and our work lives in order to continue to grow and reclaim our sense of self. There are certain periods in our life where we are confronted with the choice to remain secure in a situation or to break free. Some suggest that we move through seven-year cycles where we get the choice to go on growing or deepen feelings of complacency. If we bury our head in the sand, then we will be provided with another opportunity further down the road, only it is likely to be less gentle the second time around!

When this key is unlocked we will enjoy our physical existence and make the most of it. We all need some security and stability as essential 'nutrients' to provide us with continuity and connection. We feel safe when we have a certain amount of routine and structure and can take the risks we need that allow us the freedom to explore and grow. Once we become overly attached to the material world to give us security we lose our authentic power and can end up feeling desperately insecure. We surround ourselves with more of everything and yet never feel the freedom to really enjoy life.

> John and Sandra had worked hard in their early life and accumulated a good deal of wealth. They owned a large home and several expensive cars. They both had closets full of designer clothes and Sandra's jewellery collection was exceptional. They had installed a state-of-the-art security system and had dogs and minders.
>
> Over the years as they acquired more and more material wealth Sandra found herself less and less willing to leave her home, afraid that someone might steal something. She only went out for a few hours at a time and

> insisted that family and friends come to her. By the time she was in her late thirties she was rarely seen in the local town but continued to acquire new possessions from catalogues and personal visits from leading fashion houses.
>
> It took the death of a loved one for her to realise that she had lost touch with what was important. Her sense of identity and security depended on what she owned. 'I sold my soul for what I thought would bring me contentment and instead I became a prisoner of my possessions.' Today she and John have found a new kind of security and are travelling a good deal, enjoying their lives in new and different ways that bring them a sense of freedom.

If on the other hand we become overly attached to freedom we can find ourselves feeling deeply insecure in other ways. There are dangers if we have insufficient roots in the physical world and are disconnected from others. When our feet don't touch the ground, it can be hard to belong anywhere. We then find ourselves moving from job to job and relationship to relationship, never really having a sense of family, or anchoring.

Often those of us who have had a difficult childhood begin a search to find the deeper belonging that wasn't there when we were younger. Having let go of a family system that we didn't really feel at home in, we move to the other end of the continuum and find ourselves out of balance, sometimes denying any need for physical security. When we do this, we can end up feeling a little like a 'lost soul', finding it hard to come back to earth and get grounded. For as long as we remain marginal we will feel like outsiders to the groups around us. We have difficulty freeing up the vital force that allows us to join with others and enjoy the wonders of being fully human.

Freedom and security can be elusive. As we connect to the voice of our soul's authority we find it easier to create balance and to contribute our full leadership potential in this changing world.

The Value of Non-violence

Survival is a basic instinct and from the perspective of the animal part of our natures it's an issue of survival of the fittest. However, we are a lot more than this and as we grow we have the opportunity to claim our true potential as co-creators. We seek ways to break the cycle that perpetuates violence in all its forms.

When this Key is in the locked position we can feel fearful or insecure and find the increasing levels of violence in the world a threat to our own survival. As a result we tend to look outside ourselves to identify those who we think are to blame for making us feel this way. Much of the violence we see around us today comes from deep-rooted patterns of insecurity and an absence of belonging. For this to change we each need to look at the big and little ways in which we violate ourselves and others by what we think, feel and do!

As we go through life we can lose touch with what is best for us, giving away our authentic power in exchange for a sense of quasi-belonging. We enter family and job situations that we know deep down are not good for us and we end up getting stuck. Some of these relationships promote physical and emotional violence and we get caught up in patterns of abuse. Sometimes we stay because it's familiar – at least we know where we stand, and even though it isn't healthy we fear the insecurity that comes from stepping into the unknown. The saying 'better the devil you know than the devil you don't' keeps us locked into situations that subvert our authentic leadership power.

Whether we are the victim or the perpetrator of these violations, the cost to who we are is high. Embracing the value of non-violence, however, requires focusing on more than just the physical world. Once we adopt the alliance mindset of interconnectedness, we become aware that it is our thoughts as well as our behaviours that have an impact on the larger whole. Gandhi was a masterful teacher in showing us the power of non-violence.

When we think, feel or act in ways that promote non-violence we are demonstrating the depth of our inner security. As human beings we will inevitably find ourselves in situations that challenge our ego's survival. How we resolve them will depend on our self-awareness and how clearly we understand the assumption that if somebody loses, nobody wins. A commitment to non-violence on every level becomes an essential first step to strengthening both inner and outer security and taking authentic leadership.

Taking Better Care of Ourselves

Most of us have room for improvement in caring for ourselves and our physical well-being. Whether it's the food we eat, the hours we keep or the exercise we don't take, many of our feelings of security depend on the state of our health. When we lose sight of the fact that our body is essential to serving our soul's intention we find ourselves failing to honour it in respectful ways. Some of us will wait until our health breaks down or we are emotionally out of balance before we actually acknowledge we're out of sorts.

When energy is not flowing properly through this centre we find ourselves experiencing stress-related disorders such as constipation, bladder infections, lower back pain or stiffness and 'lazy legs'. We will also experience physical imbalances that can cause mood swings and feelings of insecurity. Eating too much spicy food, drinking too much alcohol and indulging our sweet tooth can cause excess heat in the body and lead us to feeling angry and irritable. Lack of sleep or too much dry or raw food can lead some of us to feel anxious and insecure. Too much stodgy food and not enough exercise can lead us to feeling apathetic and stuck.

Today, more and more of us are placing the issue of life balance higher on our personal agendas. We are learning how to take care of ourselves and are becoming increasingly aware of the need to establish equilibrium in a world where the demand on our energy is increasing daily. When we take responsibility for both our physical and psychological well-being, removing ourselves from situations that deplete us and creating ones that are energising, we immediately feel more secure. Sometimes it's really easy to take back the power we have given away to others and onto whom we project our insecurities. It just takes self-awareness and a willingness to break old habits that no longer have any value.

Change and Life

When we follow the rhythm of life we find ourselves alternating between stability and change. These always confront us with opportunities to deepen our sense of inner security. A house move or a change in a spouse or partner rattles our sense of belonging and causes us to feel uprooted. So too does a change of job, or the death of someone close to us. It also gives us the chance to strengthen the roots inside ourselves and renew our commitment to living authentically.

Some of us try to lessen the impact of change by avoiding making commitments in the first place. Afraid of settling down (and sometimes of growing up), we are constantly on the move. In this way we never become attached or dependent, and therefore never have to suffer the pain of letting go. Change becomes the life we know and is the only constant.

By continuously changing our outer reality we fail to find what Richard Leider refers to as 'a sense of place' for ourselves in the world. We simply keep moving: we never allow the grass to grow under our feet and we make a home for ourselves wherever we are. We never have to risk abandonment because we never stay anywhere or remain in relationships long enough to feel any sense of deep connection to anyone or anything outside ourselves. When we do find ourselves desirous of stability, and in most cases we will, our life of perpetual change then becomes the status quo we have to release!

A strong sense of inner security comes from honouring the shifting needs within ourselves. There will be times in our life when we feel the need to remain stable and other times when we are ripe to make change. As we become more self-aware we release our attachment to one or the other and allow ourselves to be guided by an inner sense of what is needed. We also allow others the freedom to make their own choices in alignment with the rhythm of their life.

Key Questions

- What does 'being secure' mean to you?
- Where may you be too comfortable in your life? And what is it costing you?
- How do you support others to find an inner sense of security?
- What are some of the core beliefs you live by? Are they your own?
- In what ways do you take care of your physical well-being? Is it enough?
- How does the 'fear of abandonment' hold you back?

Organisational Implications

If we place too much emphasis on physical security and the need to belong within an organisation, we will see the extreme examples of compliance leadership. This creates environments where people are afraid to offer a point of view that is different from the group's because of their fear of being seen as 'the odd one out'. The desire for approval and the need to remain secure in a job stops them from expressing their authentic leadership power. Nobody dares to challenge the way things are and there is little or no room for deviation from the norm. If we want to grow, we may have to make some tough choices and separate ourselves from the ties that bind us to situations that inhibit personal risk-taking.

Some organisational cultures are unconsciously abusive of their people, promoting levels of insecurity that lead employees to work long hours and sacrifice other parts of their lives in order to feel safe in their positions. The workload is so demanding that employees are pressured to achieve unrealistic expectations. 'Bully bosses' expect their employees to put their work above everything, saying: 'If they burn out then that's just too bad, they obviously didn't have what it takes.' Fortunately this attitude is not widespread and as people become more secure in themselves there is less tolerance of this kind of behaviour.

Awareness of the value of life-balance to the organisation's bottom line has been increasing over the past decade or so. Conscientious employers provide opportunities for more flexible hours and facilities where people can exercise and take care of themselves within the workplace. People everywhere are beginning to recognise that a one-dimensional approach to life diminishes our sense of deeper security rather than enhancing it.

> In a recent meeting in Europe, a group of executives talked for many hours about the need to create more time for their personal lives and for physical exercise. They were feeling high levels of stress because of the constant changes with which they were dealing within their organisation. All of them admitted that it was their family and themselves who suffered, and they were going home at night exhausted. Some spoke of the extent to which their personal lives had deteriorated and how they were feeling a 'hollowness' to their success. They found little time for personal reflection and to recharge their batteries. As a result they were feeling lower energy levels and a loss of balance.

The Importance of Anchors

In recent years, the significance of this leadership Key in all kinds of organisations has become more apparent as a result of downsizing. Before this time people could find security and connection to others from their jobs or their work life. Today, this outer physical security is not always there. Ironically, in many cases it is not present in the family environment either, leaving many feeling abandoned and sometimes betrayed by the institutions they believed would provide them with a sense of belonging.

Unless those in leadership roles are skilled in encouraging healthy levels of inner security and establishing strong connections in times of change, it is unlikely that people will remain very productive. Attention to group dynamics and issues of inclusion need to be understood to ensure cohesion. A lot of organisations are suffering because their people no longer have any sense of loyalty to their employers. They feel insecure and separate from one another, and self-interest or the WIIFM syndrome ('what's in it for me?') takes over. At times of uncertainty, it is a leadership imperative to provide people with help in identifying both personal and organisational anchors in order for them to feel secure and grounded.

One critical organisational anchor that is often undervalued in these situations is the need for higher levels of visibility of those who are in key leadership roles. Nothing beats personal contact with someone who has influence when there is a lot of insecurity about, provided these people are authentic. Unfortunately, because of an absence of relationship skills at higher levels of management, and because of the pressure on short-term results, this doesn't always happen enough. The result is a loop that is constantly reinforcing – because people don't feel secure and respected, productivity goes down and survival is threatened.

> The management team of a large organisation had been working long and hard to put together comprehensive plans for a reduction in force. It was the first time that anything of this magnitude had ever happened to this well-established corporation. Other people knew something was going on but were unaware of the details. The members of the management team found the task extremely wrenching, especially when it went from purely a numbers exercise to naming the people on the list. They agonised for hours and days, afraid of the consequences on both the individuals and the organisation as a whole.
>
> By the time it came to roll out the plans, they had bought into it, regained their objectivity and were ready to get things implemented. They had forgotten how they had felt when they first heard what had to be done. They were operating in their usual 'let's get on with the job' ways. The resistance from the rest of the organisation was significant and the insecurity was high. People felt destablised, like the rug had been pulled out from underneath them. There was

> a good deal of resentment at the invisibility and insensitivity of the leadership.
>
> Some of the management team began to realise that this process needed to be handled with greater care than they had ever thought necessary. They were at risk of losing the goodwill not only of those who were leaving but of those who would stay. They became more available and more open, and saw that a key part of their task was to facilitate the overall change process and not simply to implement it. At the same time as helping people to let go of the past, they had to actively build a platform for the future.

With a firm foundation and a strong leadership presence, people find it easier to function and to roll with the changes. Even if the structures are temporary, as long as they can feel a sense of belonging they will perform more effectively. An important part of leadership today is to facilitate change and to encourage people to strengthen their inner security and find more roots inside themselves. They need help to get in touch with their personal values and to release attachment to outdated patterns and beliefs. In this way, people let go of some of their dependency on the external world and are better able to cope with increasing levels of uncertainty, while still feeling secure.

The capabilities listed below are associated with this Leadership Key, and are paramount if organisations want to continue to inspire growth in today's environment.

Leadership Capabilities

- Promote work–life balance
- Build connection and belonging
- In touch with personal values
- Challenge outdated beliefs
- Able to create temporary structures at times of change

- Set clear ground rules and understand group dynamics
- Are willing to let go and release attachment

Global Implications

If we look at the leadership challenge of establishing security through 'global glasses', we can see the enormity of the task we are facing. The world is seriously out of balance. There are billions of people living below the poverty level and whose basic needs for survival are not being met. The increase in terrorist activity and the growing crisis in the Middle East threaten the security of the world. Some of those in significant leadership roles are still stuck in patterns of strong self-interest and are willing to go to extremes to protect their superiority, while many more are becoming increasingly aware that war in an interdependent society destroys rather than establishes security. Nobody wins!

A New Identity

In order to feel secure and have a sense of identity, people need a sense of belonging to a culture, a nationality or some sort of ethnic rooting, and this will always be the case. Today, as we transition to a global society it is important to create a broader sense of identity and belonging – that of being human. If, as we move forward, we allow our differences to separate us and we lose the common sense of humanity, we will continue to create unnecessary risks to our collective survival. War, famine, global warming, poverty and many diseases are all forms of 'violence' that result from our collective patterns of thoughts, feelings and behaviours. With a new consciousness and a shared value base we can reduce and even eradicate much of this. The Seven Keys help us to find ways to expand our thinking and reconnect to a deeper sense of our interrelatedness.

Although we are still witnessing the destruction of many of the species that provide the foundation for our physical well-being as a human family, people are realising that the future is not sustainable if we continue as we have in the past. Pollution, depletion of the ozone layer and exhaustion of non-renewable resources are beginning to affect us all, no matter where we live. The absence of awareness of the connection between economics, ecology and humanity, coupled with short-termism and parochial thinking, is no longer excusable. We all have access to great quantities of information and are less willing to support leaders who are not looking at a bigger picture. People are beginning to take the leadership into their own hands to help contribute to securing the well-being of the whole.

> Twenty-two-year-old Hannabeth Luke survived the Bali bombing in October 2002, but she lost her soul-mate. She describes how her perspective has changed as a result of her experience. 'When I used to hear about terrorism and war on the news, my attitude was always: "That's terrible but there's nothing I can do." Then this happened and I thought: "This is my problem, it's everybody's responsibility. It's about inequality, how the world is run – and it's especially up to young people like me to make a difference."'

The *Relationship Age* is here and many people are recognising that we have to live very differently as a global society if we are to ensure our future survival. Becoming familiar with the characteristics of this leadership Key, and gaining a deeper understanding of the importance of Establishing Security inside ourselves first, is a critical step in accessing authentic leadership. Once we have secure roots within ourselves and in the physical world we are able to get in touch with our inner power and the rich energy awaiting us when we turn the next Key.

7 □

GENERATING PASSION

Pleasure and emotions are the root of desire.
Through desire we create movement.
Through movement we create change.
Consciousness thrives on change.
Anodea Judith PhD

THE SECOND KEY

Characteristics
Unlocked
Creative, self-sufficient, sexually alive, adventurous, physically and emotionally intimate, playful, dynamic, personal risk-taker
Locked
Low self-worth, sexual fears and boredom, frustrated, overindulgent, static, lacking creativity, over-controlling, dependent on addictive substances or behaviours

Personal Implications

THE POTENT ENERGY OF this second Key has a lot to do with connecting with our ability to be co-creators and to generate new worlds for ourselves, personally and collectively. The fundamental force of this leadership Key has to be well understood if we are to truly inspire a new orientation to leadership and claim our authentic power. When the energy of this centre is free and operating in healthy ways it allows us to experience our creative potential by giving birth to new ideas, as well as the delights of sexual union, and giving birth to the next generation. When we focus our attention here we get in touch with the experience of desire, and we say: 'I want.' We seek ways to gratify those desires and discover the pleasures of satisfying our sexual and sensual natures.

Once we have a firm rooting within ourselves, and feel connected to the physical world, our consciousness shifts to the awareness that we are physically separate from each other. The desire then arises to overcome this feeling of separation and to join with another or others, to merge. When we awaken to the power of passion it can either be gradual, or quite dramatic if we are strongly attracted to someone else. It is a powerful force for change and can be physically and spiritually transformative when we learn to channel it properly.

It is also the energy of this Key that may lead us to be faced with major dilemmas, because we are suddenly confronted with the power of choice. We start to think differently from other members in our social, work and family groups. We use our own experience as a basis to re-evaluate some of the beliefs and assumptions we once accepted without question as true for us.

As we get in touch with our passion we can get caught in a clash of values and ideology, and have to choose between remaining secure and rooted where we have always been, or to risk the adventure that comes from embarking on a journey of soul-discovery. Our physical roots will always remain with us; however, the attachment to them begins to change.

If we are to claim our authentic leadership power and tap into our co-creative potential, the chances are we will have to 'leave home'. There are many of us who move hundreds of miles from our families of origin and have families of our own, yet have never really 'left home'. It is not as simple as it sounds and we sometimes find it easier to continue to live with a set of assumptions that keep life safe and predictable, rather than to allow our passion and accept the challenge to change.

The Pull of Opposites

This Second Key deals with the attraction of opposites, resulting in the release of the energy needed to ignite the life force within us.

It is both generative and destructive and unlocks a potent energy full of change and creative tension. Only a few years ago, it would have been hard to imagine people in business and politics talking about 'generating passion' as a key leadership quality. Yet the only two words on the front cover, other than the title, of the AT&T Wireless Annual Report 2002 were 'passion' and 'performance'. Today this critical relationship between passion and achievement is a subject that is often discussed, as management seeks to revitalise the workplace.

Normally, when we think of passion, it is in relation to sexual expression and the desire to satisfy the yearnings of a physical and emotional nature. It is seen as the coming together of two people who, when they find each other, catalyse an energy that can lead them to achieve things that they could not do alone. They discover the power of creative synergy and the extraordinary gifts that come from such an attraction. This can be the beginning of a life-long alliance in supporting each other's soul's journey if connected to the heart energy of the Fourth Key.

The energy of the Second Key influences our *relationships with one another* in the same way that the energy of the first centre influences our relationships with groups. Once we have identities that are separate from the group, we are able to connect more closely with other individuals and to explore deeper truths about ourselves.

Part of the challenge we face in such relationships is in being able to both merge and enjoy the experience of 'union' and to separate, so as to maintain our unique identities. If we don't, we can find it difficult to draw emotional boundaries, and we end up placing our feelings of self-worth in the hands of others. In doing so, we reduce our potency for leadership and risk becoming overly dependent.

Often we attract, or are attracted to, our opposites in order to discover more about who we are. These people act as mirrors to us, and through the chemistry we create in such relationships we can access our creative genius. Sufi leader Pir Vilayat Khan talks about 'finding yourself in another yourself', a challenging and rewarding process if we remain conscious and take responsibility for our own projections.

All too often we project onto the other person those parts of ourselves that we haven't learned to accept, in other words our disowned or shadow energies. If we don't recognise that the other person is merely reflecting aspects of ourselves that we haven't yet integrated, we can feel misunderstood and become over-controlling making the other person out to be a hero or a villain. It is this same attraction that draws us into business partnerships as well as close friendships.

> Sarah was in her mid-twenties when she met Alan. They were strongly attracted to each other – it was love at first sight. She admired his charm and creative outlook while he liked her strong take-charge attitude. He was much more easygoing and playful and she was the responsible one who provided the structure and took care of the details. For a while their passion flowed and they balanced each other perfectly, but then she began to be resentful – he seemed to be having lots of fun and she was the one who had to be serious.
>
> Alan was finding that Sarah was becoming more and more controlling and their relationship began to suffer big time. What had attracted them initially was that they had seen the opposite in each other and together felt like they were two halves of the same whole. However, as time went on this didn't satisfy either of them, because instead of seeing the need to integrate the opposite within themselves they chose to blame each other for their feelings. They then ended up polarising their positions and found it difficult to find the harmony in their relationship because they were unable to find the balance within themselves.

The energy associated with this leadership Key challenges us to become conscious of duality and to work with these powerful opposing forces in ways that bring about acts of creation. Instead of projecting our underdeveloped parts onto others, expecting them to take care of 'it' for us, we have to learn ways of integrating all the diverse aspects within our selves. When we do we are able to tap into our creative genius coming together with others to learn and make a bigger contribution rather than to expect them to make us whole.

Unfortunately, in Western society this energy is often misunderstood, promoting unnecessary levels of competitiveness and control. There is little education for children on the nature of this source of vitality and its expression beyond simply the sexual act itself. This leads either to its suppression with a resulting loss of creativity or, to a misdirection of the energy into the external world. Much of the meaningless violence and the ineffectiveness of leadership in our society today grows out of our inability to come to terms with this vital inner drive and to understand its relationship to our emotions.

The Value of Purpose

Many people of all ages are full of feelings they are unable to express in healthy ways because of an absence of understanding. Instead they burn off this energy either by vandalism or by acts of sexual violence and perversion. Alternatively they suppress this powerful force of creation and destruction, and not knowing how to control their inner urges, they turn to addictive substances, like alcohol and drugs.

Commitment to the spiritual value of *purposefulness* is essential to focusing our authentic leadership power if this energy is to be of value. Passion is a primary source of our power to create and to destroy. It has been the driving force behind most of the significant changes in human history. If focused in ways to serve a higher purpose, passion becomes the fuel for achieving extraordinary results. When we feel passionate about life and engage our hearts in the process, we experience a stronger sense of self-worth, because we're switched on to life. When we don't, we start to lose this vital energy and feel apathy and self-doubt. Passion without purpose can lead to unrealistic desires, strong attachments and misguided acts of destruction, ultimately causing pain and suffering.

The *fear of loss of control* belongs to the Second Key. It is what keeps many people stuck in leadership patterns of the past, and away from forming the close bonds with others that allow transformation to happen. Instead of creating environments of openness and experimentation, these people end up controlling everything and everyone. When we don't allow ourselves to express the emotional desires of this centre and face this fear, we give up control in other ways. Dependence on alcohol, tobacco, sugar or working too much grows out of the absence of healthy expressions of this energy in purposeful ways.

Some of us, when we lose sight of our broader life purpose, unknowingly allow our work to control us. Sometimes it's because we are unwilling or unable to deal with the feelings that arise in our lives and relationships. Other times it can simply be the inability to draw healthy boundaries between our offices and our homes. The result is the same. We begin to sacrifice our creativity and lose some of the passion in our lives. We end up having little time or energy for sexual expression other than simply the release of tension. This second centre begins to function sub-optimally and we lose power. When this happens, we are vulnerable to periods of depression and to stress-related health risks in the areas associated with the sexual organs.

There are many people today who equate leadership with being available to their business twenty-four hours a day. They become married to their jobs, and are paying a high price, having lost touch with their families and the deeper yearnings of their soul. Some admit they are afraid to slow down and take a look inside, not knowing what they may find. Others just rationalise this behaviour away, seeing it as 'part of the package'. However, without a higher sense of life purpose we dilute our authentic power, becoming reactive to everything around us and eventually running out of juice.

Much of our sense of self-worth comes from our ability to be generative – it is why we are here. Creation is our birthright, and if we don't express our passion we remain unfulfilled. In leadership development activities over the years, I have asked people to raise their hands if they think they are creative in some way. I am always surprised at how few people acknowledge their power to create. I am also saddened because I know only too well the restrictions that prevent us from 'having fun once we grow up', because of the perceived need to keep our feelings under control.

Many of these barriers unknowingly end up becoming self-imposed and self-reinforcing. We buy into them as part of our early programming and they remain with us unconsciously. If we are to re-ignite our passion and take our authentic leadership power we have to challenge our outdated assumptions, establish our own independent beliefs and follow a purposeful path.

Building and sustaining high-quality one-to-one relationships with others is an important aspect of maintaining this vitality for life. These relationships provide the safety to express our feelings and to be authentic. In doing so, we release the emotional blocks that can get in the way of our progress and that sometimes hold us back from taking on leadership roles. Once we have opened up emotionally, our passion to create expands beyond belief, and life becomes full of both risk and opportunity!

Key Questions

- What turns you on to life?
- Which emotions are hard and which are easy for you to express?
- How well do you live with ambiguity and uncertainty?
- What do you do to manage conflict in healthy ways?
- How well do you build connections with others?
- What is your life purpose? How are you living it?
- How might 'fear of loss of control' get in your way?

Organisational Implications

In twenty-five years of working in organisations, it has become clear to me that there is an incredible natural resource that remains untapped. The potential wealth of creativity is enormous and yet outdated patterns of leadership behaviour keep it in the shadows. There is an underlying fear of loss of control if people begin to release this powerful energy in the workplace. However, passion focused in the service of a higher purpose can bring exceptional levels of performance and free the creative spirit in ways that inspire excellence.

In the more traditional organisations, the leadership orientation associated with the compliance mindset coupled with the sheer weight of structure prevent people from accessing this creative genius. Passion and creativity come from bringing together opposites, from the synthesis of diverse points of view and from creative synergies. Many of these organisations are still one-dimensional, with an emphasis on conformity, and a low tolerance for diversity.

Companies are paying high prices for not opening themselves to the opportunities that arise when you bring different cultures, genders and ideologies together. We know that forty per cent of the *Fortune* 500 companies that existed in 1983 do not exist in the same form today, as a result of mergers, acquisitions and bankruptcies, but do we know the deeper reasons why? Could it be that many were unable to generate the passion they needed to continually regenerate themselves? With so much homogeneity perhaps their ideas became stale and they began to stagnate.

There is growing recognition for the need to overcome resistance to change and to encourage greater diversity. Managements are realising they need the emotional sparks that come from different perspectives, united behind a common purpose. Without the interaction of opposites, life and work become mundane and repetitive, draining our energy rather than charging us up.

Many corporations today are discovering that they have little diversity in terms of age, gender or culture in their top leadership teams. They're recognising that they are not the most exciting places to be; and that if they continue in this way, they will limit their potential growth. Some are already finding it difficult to attract and retain the bright newcomers who are worldlier, and who are looking for fertile fields in which to nurture their creative ideas.

The establishment of environments that support differences, and where women and men from diverse cultures can express their authenticity, has to be a critical leadership priority in any global organisation. When people who are different work together in respectful relationships they inspire each other, stretch and test each other, and come to trust each other. They engage in healthy conflict and are able to create in ways that a single-gender or monocultural group is unable to do.

> Chris was forty-two when his eldest son died suddenly. He had never known such pain. 'I always kept my feelings pretty much to myself and had no idea how emotional I could be.' He surprised himself by the depth of feeling he experienced and how it opened him up to a very different way of seeing life. He had been successful in his career as a chemical engineer and was in a senior management position when his world turned upside down. The organisation decided not to move him as planned, recognising that the transition he was facing was already significant.
>
> He described the changes he went through as mind-blowing. 'It cracked me wide open and I realised at one point that I had to make a choice. I could sink into the desperation and despair or make some meaning out of what had happened to Colin.' Chris chose the second option and after going through the deepest part of the transition he emerged with a renewed sense of purpose. He decided to focus his energy on the issue of diversity in the workplace. He wanted to see more women and people of colour in management roles and became a pioneer in attracting girls into science. As a strong advocate for women's issues he became a champion of diversity throughout his company, placing it firmly on the corporate agenda. The energy freed

up by his inner process following the loss of his son became the source of a great deal of purposeful activity. It gave Chris a passion and a focus that changed the entire meaning of his life.

Change and Diversity

Creativity means change and change means growth. It also means possible loss of control. When you bring opposites together, there is tension. That tension creates emotion, and that emotion generates energy. It's exciting and risky. It requires an understanding of polarity and the willingness to work with paradox. It takes us out of our comfort zones and raises issues of difference, and the possibilities for confrontation. However without it, there's repetition, and stagnation. With too much of it, there are untold levels of chaos and confusion! This is the Key where duality rules supreme. It presents us with the opportunity for acknowledging and harmonising the opposites that generate both our inner and outer tensions.

The leadership challenge in the creative process is, paradoxically, to provide enough structure to allow freedom. Without any order there will be wild and aimless activity. With too much there will be nothing new, just a repeat of the past. A clear sense of purpose can ignite the passion organisations need to be successful.

In companies that are beginning to operate with an alliance mindset and that have developed more of a project team approach, it is more common to see the use of 'purpose' rather than structure to maintain cohesion and focus. By developing strong networks of relationships as the means of connection, ground rules are developed for working together in ways that encourage authentic self-expression. Some organisations have introduced what Swedish consultant Urban Berggren calls 'punishment-free zones', supporting people in expressing their feelings without fear of negative consequences.

The introduction of the balanced scorecard is also helping people increase their awareness of the many polarities inherent in maintaining healthy organisations. Such an approach encourages short- and long-term thinking, a focus on results as well as development and the establishment of both quantitative and qualitative performance measures.

Mergers and acquisitions are also putting pressure on organisations to open up to diverse points of view and new leadership behaviours, although many are still struggling. A major factor that has contributed to the failure of mergers has simply been the inability of management to promote creative synergy. Instead of valuing diversity and promoting partnership, the dominant culture simply takes over, putting a lid on the potential for creativity and leaving many people feeling impotent.

When people are competent at working with this Key (capable of both generating and focusing passion in productive ways), the emotional energy that is freed up becomes a wonderful source of bright new ideas and products. Emotion is all about the movement of energy. When it is not expressed it causes blocks to the natural flow of creative energy on both individual and organisational levels.

As the number of mergers, alliances, and acquisitions increases, the importance of leadership based on authentic expression must be evoked to work with these powerful energies of opposition. The skills and capabilities for unlocking the energy of the Second Key are listed below, and there is plenty of room for their development in organisations today!

Leadership Capabilities

- Sets clear personal boundaries
- Able to create meaning and purpose
- Engages emotionally
- Encourages diversity and tolerates ambiguity
- Looks to build partnerships and alliances
- Initiates and embraces change
- Deals well with dilemmas and conflict
- Takes risks and has fun

Global Implications

The need for creativity, for valuing diversity, for building alliances and for working consciously with these potent Second Key energies has never been more necessary. The way forward in a global society is to focus on bringing together diverse people and ideologies in ways that promote creative synergies.

War, inner-city violence, rapes and other atrocities are all indications of our failure to do this, and reflect the limitations of the existing orientation to leadership. Interestingly, most of the fighting today is not about conquering and acquiring bigger territories. It is conflicts of ideology, of values, beliefs and cultural and ethnic differences.

Three of the most lucrative 'businesses' in the world today are weapons, drugs and illegal immigration. This suggests that many of us are either afraid of or wanting to escape from our current realities, physically, psychologically or emotionally. If such realities are allowed to continue unabated, the prognosis for the future is not good, and simply fighting against it only reinforces the vicious cycle.

A Question of Balance

As a global society, we are seriously out of balance. There is too much inequity between the North and the South, the East and the West and many different ethnic groups to create a sustainable future. We need to examine the patterns that have grown out of our pasts, overcome our fears of loss of control and transform our consciousness if we are to redress these imbalances.

The lack of balance that exists today between masculine and feminine energies on a global level is significant. A masculine orientation to leadership of territorialism, domination, aggression, competition and acquisition, if allowed to remain unchecked, will undoubtedly lead to our demise. The more feminine leadership orientation of connection, integration, compassion, cooperation and contribution has to rise to stand equal to the masculine, in order to bring about the necessary changes.

The extraordinary potency that is yielded when all these

energies come together within each of us is what will generate the expression of authentic leadership needed on a global level. The opportunity to create a future of peace and plenty is there for us all if we will only allow the creative opportunities to emerge, and respect, rather than resist, those who are different from us.

The Second Key frees us to enjoy the passion and adventure that come from allowing ourselves to be co-creators of new thought forms and new realities. It awakens us to the potential we all have to be generative and to bring the masculine and feminine qualities together within ourselves. Paradoxically, it is only through honouring our diversity that we will create the foundation for global unity.

SHARING POWER

All power to accomplish flows through relationship.
Mark Yeoell

THE THIRD KEY

Characteristics
Unlocked
Powerful, self-determining, enthusiastic, strong, autonomous, confident, purposeful, assertive, encouraging and bold
Locked
Low self-esteem, blaming, victim, submissive, harsh, fearful, resentful, feelings of shame and guilt, domineering, aggressive and insensitive

Personal Implications

THIS CENTRE IS THE SEAT of our personal will, without which we are unable to access the full potential of our authentic leadership power. The Third Key opens the door to the primary source of our feelings of self-esteem and the strength of belief we have in ourselves. When we turn our attention here we begin the deeper journey of soul-discovery. We shift our perspectives from focusing primarily on the outside world, and start to work with the riches of our inner realities.

The First Key provides us with our sense of rooting and connection. The Second Key wakes up our creativity and physical desires. The Third Key unlocks the wish to turn our dreams into reality. It is about action, self-empowerment and the use of our will to express our uniqueness. Here we start a more conscious exploration of the *relationship to the Self.*

As our self-awareness and self-worth increase, we begin to develop our true identity separate from others. We have the opportunity to take leadership and hold ourselves accountable for the ways we think and behave. We assert ourselves, believing that we have the right to our own point of view, even if it is at odds with those with whom we once agreed. We risk being different from the crowd and have renewed determination to fulfil our dreams and our desires.

Unlocking the energy associated with this leadership Key often requires an act of will that causes us to turn our backs on the known and comfortable and set out on what M. Scott Peck refers to as 'the Road Less Travelled'. It is only when we have claimed the identity of our real Self that we can access the deeper desires of the soul, and our authentic power. *Fear of rejection* can hold us back from accessing our true will and claiming our potential for leadership.

Some of us unknowingly block the truth of who we are, either because of painful childhood memories, or because of an absence of self-acceptance. Others make a conscious choice not to reveal ourselves, in order to secure approval from others. Preferring not to risk the rejection of others, we can end up rejecting ourselves, and in so doing lose our right to happiness as human beings. We withhold our natural expressions and comply with the desires of those around us. Gradually, our power for authentic leadership weakens as we forfeit our enthusiasm for life, losing touch with who we are and what we want.

We give away our power every time we say we're doing something we don't really want to do, either because we feel we 'must', we 'should', we 'ought to' or we 'have to,' rather than saying, 'I am making a conscious choice to do or not do this.' When we go against our own will and are not emotionally honest, staying in relationships or situations to keep someone else happy, we are giving up the power to take leadership of our lives. Feelings of shame, guilt, resentment and depression all too often accompany this sense of compromise.

There are many things that drain our will, such as our fears, our emotional attachments, too much focus on the past or the future and self-criticism. What's important is to be conscious of our energy rhythms and to look for the sources of depletion. This can only be done if we are in touch with our inner world. All too often we accept failing levels of power and put it down to age and stress, never really taking control of the factors that are depleting our vital energy. If this goes on too long and becomes a chronic condition, a small change may send us over the edge into despair. At this point we sometimes question our will to live and can engage in self-destructive behaviours, with suicide becoming a very real option for some, as the ultimate act of self-rejection.

Definitions of Power

In our society, the concept of power is often misunderstood. Some people believe power to be negative, linking it with domination and control. Others see it as related to wealth and status. Some feel they don't have enough of it and want more, while others deny that they even want it, let alone have it! Some appear powerful on the outside to protect an inner lack of confidence, while others are living examples of this little saying: 'There is nothing as strong as real gentleness and nothing as gentle as real strength.'

'Power' is a term loaded with values and assumptions that have grown out of people's life experiences. Power is neither positive nor negative. It is energy. The way that we express it is what makes the difference. Gandhi told us: 'Power, privilege and position are great resources. Use them well. Do not become attached to them, for when we do, we begin to lose our moral fibre.'

It can help to understand power if we look at it through three lenses:

- The Power of Position — We have influence because we have *status.*
- The Power of Possession — We have influence because we have *material wealth.*
- The Power of Presence — We have influence because we are *authentic.*

Looking at the concept of power through the third lens is what this new orientation to leadership is all about. With such a perspective, our focus shifts from being more outer directed to being internally guided. Presence is all about 'pres(enting one's ess)ence', the inner riches of who we are – our soul's expression. If we are to take leadership, we have to develop enough self-esteem and authenticity to be unafraid to let down the facade that keeps us from being seen.

In some cases, this can be quite frightening to do. It is especially true if we have been hurt in our early years or are holding on to secrets that we want to keep from others. Whenever we make the commitment to live true to ourselves, we risk the chance that others may not approve of us and we may find ourselves alone for a while.

Someone who has been the initiator in a divorce or the breakup of a relationship, or who has left their family of origin, their religion or even their profession, knows only too well the courage it takes to break through theses fears of disapproval. Sometimes it is others that try to make us feel ashamed or guilty of the choices we have made. When we are accepting enough of ourselves and are committed to living authentically, we will be able to see that these are *their* issues and we can *choose* not to take them too personally.

> Bill was an accountant. He had been an accountant for twenty years but what he really wanted to do was to be a farmer. He was feeling very stressed and his doctor had told him he needed to do some serious re-evaluation of his life. He didn't feel like he was living his own dream. He wanted to quit his job and move to the country. Even in his little garden in the city he had grown all sorts of vegetables and loved being outside in the open air. The office was like a prison to him.
>
> In looking back at the reason for his choices it was easy to see why he had taken this path. His father had always encouraged him to follow in his footsteps and to take on the same profession, and he had done so. Bill knew that if he continued to practise accountancy it would cost

him dearly. It took a good deal of courage for him to face his elderly father and make a different choice. After he had done so he felt an enormous sense of freedom. He was surprised at the relative ease of confronting his father with his change in direction. He had thought it would be a major power struggle, but his fear of rejection was mostly unfounded.

The power of presence brings us into 'present' time and is the only place authentic power exists. Many of us lose our potency because we have so much energy still invested in the past or projected onto the future. We have developed wonderful strategies that prevent us being fully in the here and now. Every time we talk about the past or the future our energy leaves the present moment. Of course it is vital to honour where we have been and to acknowledge where we are going – but not to dwell there.

It is so seductive to cling to the past and what has been because it is known. It is tempting to live in the future world of what could be, because we can imagine it the way we want. If we live in the present we touch both the simplicity and complexity of life as it is – the place where our past meets our future. For some of us this is a place of pain and the desire is to escape it. When we fail to connect to the natural flow of our energy and try to avoid facing 'what is' here and now, we begin to shut down the enthusiasm that fuels our sense of joie de vivre.

The true essence of power lives only in the present and is why when we are in touch with the power of our authentic presence we are an inspiration to others. When we call all our energy back from any thoughts and feelings that are caught up in the past and the future, we land powerfully in the present. We are simply defined by this moment in time with no desire to be anywhere else except here and now.

Our authentic leadership power, the power of our presence, provides us with the vital force we need to make our unique contribution in the world. If we abdicate this power, we become more vulnerable to handing over the control of our lives and our destinies to someone else. Yoga authority Suzy Newman declared after her own struggle to understand this concept 'that not to own our power is a sin, "will" is after all a gift from God.'

When we give our power away, we are more likely to engage in the blame game, taking on the role of the victim. In the absence of owning the power of our presence, we remain in situations that are abusive, and in doing so we cease to have control of our lives. In time, handing over the authorship of our lives leads us to stop nourishing ourselves, and can result in digestive disorders. If we embrace our power and connect it to divine Will (the essence of the Fifth Key) we open ourselves to the higher energies available to us on our spiritual quests. We also find our self-esteem strengthening, allowing us to assume leadership roles as sources of inspiration to others in the broader society.

Becoming 'Enough'

Accepting one's individuality is a prerequisite to sharing power. When we are at ease with our power of presence, we have a sense of respect for ourselves and find it easier to respect others. We then become less vulnerable to being controlled by someone else and have less need to control them. People who find it difficult to accept this power find themselves seeking external approval in order to get validation. As a result, they fail to take leadership responsibility and are themselves open to being manipulated by someone else's ego needs.

It would be naive to assume that owning our authentic leadership power is an easy task – it's not. To be oneself in a world that is trying to make us like everyone else is probably one of the single greatest challenges many of us will ever have to face. There are several reasons for this. *First*, there are those who may not want us to be powerful because they would lose control if we were to get in touch with our personal will. *Second*, in order to take a stand and show ourselves as we really are, we must risk rejection and the need for approval from others. *Third*, to be true to our authentic self requires us to learn to trust our intuition and relinquish attachment to external definitions of power and success.

It is a huge commitment to undertake this journey and to do

the work of reclaiming our soul's authority. To engage fully means accepting ourselves warts and all, by taking back all the energy we've invested in 'not being enough'. Sometimes we fail to take ownership of our power by handing it over to the shadow side of the 'Nuff Family'. When we are young we are bombarded with messages like you're not Oldy Nuff yet, not Biggy Nuff, not Smarty Nuff, not Toughy Nuff and every other 'Nuff' you can think of!

To move the 'not enoughs' out of our psyche means breaking through old habit patterns that have kept us 'safe' and accepted for years. When we make the statement 'I am enough,' we let go of the need for external validation, and venture into the often-uncharted territory of our inner realities. We become our own map makers and set off on a voyage full of trials and triumphs as we get in touch with our highest hopes and our deep-seated fears. These are the fears to which we have handed over the power of our presence and that have held us back from acknowledging that we alone hold the authority for our lives.

The energy centre that represents the Third Key is often thought of as the primary seat of our fears. When we are afraid, it triggers a physiological response that leads us to fight, flee or freeze. All three cause us to draw our energy inwards and to contract, tightening up our muscles so that we are ready for action. If, however, we don't deal with our fears but allow them to remain stored in our bodies and our subconscious minds instead, they can become destructive to our physical and psychological well-being, making us age and break down more rapidly. If we hold them in, they hold us back! Respecting our fears and listening to what they are trying to tell us is an important part of owning our authentic power and sharing leadership.

Power and Anger

Another significant emotion associated with this energy centre is anger. Often seen as negative, it is not always allowed to take its rightful place in our lives. This causes all sorts of issues with power and control. Anger is a core feeling and it need not be seen as either good or bad. It is a human emotion. We can choose to repress it, or we can express it in constructive or destructive ways. When we are being overly aggressive our anger is controlling us and we have given our power to the emotion. When we are asserting our needs and our wants in constructive ways, it is likely that we are making a conscious choice to be in charge of our anger.

The fundamental difference between the two expressions is that the first one is simply an emotional reaction resulting from the feeling of anger, without any consciousness about how best to channel it. The second requires us to take our power and focus this energy choicefully in ways that are transformative, and that will allow us to establish firm boundaries and clear expectations. It takes consciousness and maturity to do this and, for most of us, some experimentation and support.

If we learn how to acknowledge such feelings and then to transform them into productive energy, we will establish a trusting relationship with ourselves and with others. If on the other hand we repress our anger, we will lose some of our potential to be powerful. Anger consumes a lot of energy when allowed to remain bottled up.

The Value of Fairness

It takes daring and boldness to follow the path of our desires and ambitions with purpose and self-determination. Choosing to access our authentic leadership is not for the faint-hearted. It means liberating ourselves from the dominance of our ego and learning to trust in the power of our soul's authority. The spiritual value that underpins the Third leadership Key is *fairness*. If we are to adopt a sustainable consciousness, then equity has to be a core element. When we do not play fair and unconsciously get locked into patterns of manipulation that feed self-interest, we lose some of our leadership potency. Making a commitment to fairness requires a willingness to release some important physical, psychological and emotional attachments that have shaped our identity.

These attachments are different for all of us. They often have to do with our definitions of power and success, influencing us to behave in certain ways that lead us to cling to behaviours that are self-indulgent or self-effacing. Breaking free of these can be an enormous challenge and requires us to believe in a 'spiritual something' that is often beyond our understanding. It means jumping into the void and trusting in the unseen. It's often painful, usually exhilarating and always insightful. It is a rite of passage to our soul's source and to claiming authentic leadership.

This Third Key is the one that opens the 'outer' door to the world of spirit. It leads us to recognise that control is simply an illusion that keeps us locked into a paradigm of dominance and subservience. Waking up to this realisation is the turning point in accessing our true will and the leadership potential that is our birthright.

Once we establish our spiritual connection to a higher source of energy, we are far less influenced by the power dynamics of the outside world and also less affected by the judgements of others. We find a sense of inner security and self-esteem that supports us in taking the risks and making decisions that promote a fairer world for everyone. We become excited and enthusiastic about life and are willing to step out with our own values and beliefs and be seen for who we really are – powerful.

Key Questions

- What makes you sure you are in charge of your destiny?
- Do you let others' expectations influence you? If so, how?
- What do you do to take your power and when do you give it away?
- When are you comfortable sharing power and when are you not? Do you play fair?
- When was the last time you took a good look inside?
- How might your 'fear of rejection' hold you back?

Organisational Implications

When the energy of sharing power is functioning well in a team or organisation, there is an absence of one-up, one-down relationships. People work together towards a common goal and share the leadership according to their competencies and the needs of the task. It's fun to be part of such a group because each individual is valued. Internal competitiveness is replaced with a desire for cooperation. No single person attempts to control the situation or to dominate the process. The role of the leader is that of a focaliser and a facilitator of the collective energy, ensuring that any blocks are brought to the surface and cleared as quickly as possible.

> Rob, Susan and Jack were all business unit leaders. In some ways they were competing with each other for the next promotion. Their businesses were going through a challenging time and so they decided to bring the three operating teams together to develop some new perspectives and look for potential business synergies. It felt very risky to all of them but it was something they thought was in everyone's longer-term interest.
>
> They struggled at first over who should take the lead, as they were all self-confessed prima donnas. After some honest and open conversation they decided that maybe they could share it. Each one of them found it challenging to work in this way and yet they knew if they didn't cooperate the consequences would be costly.
>
> The results were a surprise to all of them. The process was designed to allow each of them to take responsibility for a different part of the meeting, at the same time as sharing accountability for the outcome of the whole event. They worked very effectively together in ways that they hadn't experienced before and received excellent feedback from their teams. They continued to draw on each other's expertise long after the meeting was over and were aware that it was their willingness to take a risk and share the

power that allowed them to succeed. Rob was never truly convinced that sharing leadership was a good idea, preferring to run his own show. He had to admit, however, that the benefits of the activity were far greater than he had ever anticipated.

This leadership Key is one of the most challenging in organisations today. The matrix and project-team structures that are being put in place demand more sharing of power. However, the hierarchical mindset that many managers still hold gets in the way of real change, sometimes even blocking it completely. For as long as people equate power with position or status within a hierarchical framework, and with the size of their budget or the number of people they control, the struggle to make the new organisational forms effective will continue.

Some managers develop elaborate strategic plans with all sorts of tactics designed to maintain the control of resources so as to preserve power. In some cases, bright people are given performance ratings that are lower than they deserve in order to make them less attractive to another department or division. Bosses don't want to lose their good people, because in the short term it may affect their bottom-line results and therefore their own potential for advancement.

In one organisation a senior manager told his people that if they ever left his division they would end up being disappointed. It was so clearly a veiled threat that even though he was seen as an ineffective leader, people remained with him, albeit reluctantly. Such are the dynamics of power when fear pervades. This is the shadow side of leadership, when no one is willing to face the issues and bring them out into the light.

Fortunately, there are increasing numbers of more enlightened managers who are beginning to change both their beliefs and their behaviours. Some have found that sharing power does not in fact dilute their potency, it actually expands the capacity others have for achieving higher levels of performance. This understanding makes the difference between inspirational leadership and the more traditional perspectives based on command and control. It's a wonderful paradox – the more you give it away the more you get it back.

One analogy that can be used to illustrate this concept of leadership has to do with the flame of a single candle. Imagine a group of people standing in a darkened room, each with a candle. Yours is the only one that is alight so you have a choice. You can either keep that light to yourself and lead the way, or you can invite others to light their own from yours. In doing the latter, your flame remains as strong as ever and you lose nothing except control. By sharing it you have created the opportunity for the light to expand further and further.

We can all understand this intellectually, but there are ingrained fears that prevent us from surrendering to this inner wisdom and trusting in the strength of our authentic power. Organisational reward systems also perpetuate these fears and are unknowingly reducing the capacity of employees to contribute their full leadership potential. One way all of this gets translated is in the absence of significant investment of time and rewards for mentoring and coaching. More priority is still placed on controlling resources and meeting the short-tem objectives than it is on developing the leadership potency of future generations.

Taking Accountability

The issue of accountability is frequently discussed within organisations. In the past it has sometimes been hard to identify who has the authority and responsibility for a given action. It is not uncommon for people to claim accountability for successes but to deny it when it comes to failures! Once more, the balanced scorecard approaches and new performance-management systems are beginning to correct this. Some companies are investing in succession vitality processes to create the next generation of leaders. They are introducing the needed capabilities for operating with accountability in a global environment. For these to take root, however, it will require a clear commitment by management to challenge the organisation's deeper cultural beliefs about power and control, and make the needed behaviour changes. If this doesn't happen, these processes will simply remain the flavour of the month.

The move towards 'three-sixty-degree' feedback is also a very positive step for breaking through ineffective patterns of leadership. People get insight into their performance from many different perspectives and are then given the opportunity to develop their potential. These new processes are allowing people to gain deeper understanding into their behaviours, which in turn helps them to increase their self-awareness and to take steps to strengthen their leadership competencies. It all sounds so easy, yet the reality is tough and challenges the 'old grey-suit brigade' who still walk the halls of some of the world's most powerful institutions.

> Keith and his boss didn't get along. In fact they often argued openly in meetings and clearly didn't respect each other. When it came to appraisal time Keith was able to invite some of his peers and his subordinates to give feedback on his performance. On a five-point scale his boss's answers were two points lower than the average of all the others who had rated him. It was clearly a personality clash. Keith wanted to contribute his ideas and the boss saw this as a threat to his 'position power'. He wanted to do things his way because he was the boss.
>
> With the help of the feedback Keith decided to move to another position where there was more openness to sharing ideas and therefore a greater potential to share power. He was also given some coaching to look at how his behaviour had contributed to the situation and was able to make a success of his next job.

Self-acceptance and personal empowerment are at the core of this Key. In order to take responsibility we have to claim our own authority, recognising that we are the authors of our life's experience and that we are free to move to where we can grow. Empowerment is our *will*ingness to accept responsibility, and accountability for our thoughts, our feelings and our actions. No one can empower another person. The function of authentic leadership is to create an environment where people feel competent to make informed choices and to take their power. Certain organisational climates, and the systems that support them, can be disempowering to an individual's self-expression, preventing people from taking leadership responsibility.

When empowered people come together, the energy they generate is markedly different from the classic one-up, one-down dynamic. They readily embrace the alliance mindset. The nature of relationships between 'bosses and subordinates' and 'peers and colleagues' becomes interdependence. They develop networks and project teams to facilitate a certain objective. People are connected by purpose not structure, and power is shared in ways that serve the outcome. When that purpose is fulfilled the team ends and a new team is formed to support the next objective or project.

The success of mergers, acquisitions and other such processes is also very much contingent on the ability to establish these kind of purposeful connections and facilitative structures. Whenever power becomes synonymous with structure, too much energy is invested in maintaining that structure rather than serving the needs of all the stakeholders. This is the primary reason for the blockage of energy in organisations today and why people throughout the system become frustrated and disempowered.

Building Interdependence

There are several prerequisites to interdependence:

- Unified Purpose – *A common direction and shared intent.*
- Strong Independent Partners – *Autonomous individuals who are willing to share in the interest of a common purpose.*
- Trust and Respect – *Acceptance and acknowledgement of the different perspectives that each brings and that stimulate creative synergy.*
- A Clear 'Contract' – *A clear articulation of expectations and joint development of the rules of engagement.*
- Lack of Attachment to Structure – *Recognition that structure is temporary and that purposeful relationship is the true connecting force.*

- Shared Risk and Shared Reward – *Shared accountability for results.*
- Open Mind and Open Heart – *An openness to learn and grow.*

When these conditions are present, people place value on the quality of their relationships, and perform very differently than in environments where the power structures create fear and political politeness. The human spirit by nature is generous and expansive. When people operate in a climate that supports these basic qualities, their capacity for creative contribution is unleashed.

We are all powerful beings filled with a life force that seeks to express itself in productive ways. How this energy is understood and focused makes a huge difference to the *performance health* of organisations. In today's world, the old power structures that served the industrial age have very limited value, as does the hierarchical mindset.

The leadership challenge associated with the energy of the Third Key of Sharing Power is having enough consciousness to discern when to hold the reins and when to let them go. If fear is in the driver's seat, the chances are that the power exerted will be enervating. If, on the other hand, trust is at the wheel, the power is likely to create an expansive and energising climate. The role of leadership then becomes one of generating enthusiasm, and guiding organisational and human development processes in service of the overall business purpose. These processes need to encourage people to express their authentic leadership and make decisions that result in high levels of performance excellence and self-esteem.

The following are the Leadership capabilities necessary for working with the energy of the Third Key.

Leadership Capabilities

- Takes accountability
- Shows up in full colours
- Is able to generate enthusiasm

- Honours the contribution of others
- Is unafraid of personal power
- Values differences
- Understands and focuses human energy
- Knows when to hold and when to fold

Global Implications

It is hard to imagine the kind of world we could create if we released some of our attachments to position power and possession power and trusted in the power of our presence. If we could unlock the energy that is held back as a result of the desire to accumulate wealth, the world would be a much healthier and happier place. Instead we have many of the Western advertising giants bombarding people with messages about the more you have – the bigger you are – the happier you'll be! It's unbelievable if you look at the implications on a global scale.

Some Vital Statistics

According to John D. Adams (2000), 'those 25 per cent of people alive today who live in already industrialised nations are consuming 70 per cent of the resources being used in manufacturing. As the developing countries attempt to catch up, we can expect that the demand for natural resources will also leap upward.' He explains how the net worth of the world's wealthiest 500 individuals today exceeds the world's poorest 3,000,000,000 individuals. A ratio of 6,000,000:1.

An article in *Business Week* (1992) assumed that by 2027, the global population will be approximately 11 billion. The majority of new births will be in developing nations and with the income disparity already dramatic the outlook is not encouraging. In 1960 the average income per capita in the top fifth of countries was 30 times that of the per capita of the bottom fifth. Each decade the disparity has increased: 32:1 in 1970; 45:1 in 1980; and 59:1 in 1990.

In addition, a *Business Week* study conducted in 1993 looked at what the CEOs of the largest US corporations earned in relation to their lowest-paid workers. The ratio in 1970 was 42:1, and in 1990 it was 157:1. It was further estimated in 1997 to be 200:1 and in 2000 projected to be over 400:1.

The gap between the rich and poor is increasing. If everyone begins to aspire to lives of affluence, believing that self-esteem and personal power depend on wealth and possessions, then we are clearly in trouble. We have to shift our perception of power and look inward for the deeper, more spiritual sources of success and fulfilment.

The current situation will be untenable when those who have less are no longer willing to tolerate this differential. Business in this respect has an enormous role to play. As the largest global institution, it has the power and the leadership responsibility to begin to create a world of greater fairness. By actively engaging in an exploration of the ethical values and longer-term consequences of their current operational platforms, these institutions could be instrumental in providing the leadership needed for the future well-being of humanity. Failing to do so could lead to our demise.

There is no question that this could become a win-win situation with the potential of creating healthy new markets in developing countries, but it requires a mindset that recognises the relationship between economics, ecology and sustainability, and places a higher value on the spiritual dimension of the human experience.

There are many cynics who consider business to be an institution that is depleting natural resources without any real awareness of the implications. Short-term economic gain is seen to be more important than long-term ecological sustainability and material wealth more important than the overall well-being of humanity. In some cases this is true. In others, people are waking up to the fact that we cannot continue in these ways and hope to survive.

Fortunately, there are growing numbers embracing the power of their authentic presence and taking a leadership role in the bigger picture, *especially* in the business world. The transformation that is catalysed when this Key is activated is one where we begin to look inside for the answers to life's deeper questions and claim our power to live fully in the here and now. This shift in leadership consciousness can only take place one person at a time, and as it does, the opportunity for the true Sharing of Power on a global scale becomes a possibility.

If we consider some of the most powerful people in the world in the twentieth century, in terms of their presence and their ability to influence the hearts and minds of millions of people, they would not be people of great wealth. Their power and their inspirations came from their commitments to something greater than themselves. They all risked rejection by the established order and took a stand for what they sincerely believed in: Mahatma Gandhi, Martin Luther King, John Lennon, Mother Theresa, Nelson Mandela and Vaclav Havel are all bright lights and shining examples of ordinary people with a higher purpose that embraced the value of fairness.

Letting go of the need to measure power by external criteria, and clearing away the emotional clutter that prevents us from claiming our soul's authority, are perhaps two of the toughest challenges we have to face on this path to leadership. Having the courage to trust in the power of our authentic presence and to live fully in the here and now frees us from many of the fears that hold us back.

INSPIRING LOVE

Love is the only authentic power
Caroline Myss

THE FOURTH KEY

Characteristics
Unlocked
Compassionate, forgiving, courageous, trusting, grateful, vulnerable, caring, self-accepting, liberated, expressive of sorrow, grief, joy and happiness
Locked
Lonely, aloof, hides vulnerability, self-condemning, vengeful, attached, bitter, jealous, despairing, expressive of hatred and mistrust

Personal Implications

LEADERSHIP WITHOUT LOVE is like a garden without flowers: functional, but lacking in the qualities which inspire and delight us. When our hearts are open it is easier to connect with other people. We create the capacity to experience the joy and the inspiration which give meaning to life.

This fourth energy centre provides the bridge between the material and the spiritual worlds. It is where earth (Keys 1–3) and heaven (Keys 5–7) come together in the human experience. The heart is the seat of unconditional love from which we learn the true meaning of forgiveness and compassion. It is the gateway that leads from a focus on 'doing' and 'having' to where we touch the desire 'to be'. When we turn our attention here, we begin a journey into the realm of the 'unseen' and learn to trust in a part of the self that is often beyond everyday understanding.

The first three Keys have to do with physical and emotional energy. They help us to exist in matter and form and to feel connected to a world that our five senses describe as reality. It is the part of our human existence that is tangible and that has clear structures and rules, to tell us if we are 'right or wrong'. When we unlock the energy of the Fourth Key, we take a huge leap in the acceptance of our authentic leadership power and begin to claim our spiritual inheritance.

We find ourselves asking lots of questions about the deeper meaning of life. We accept the responsibility to become the author of our own 'soul's code', a term first used by James Hillman in his book of the same name. What began as an inner journey of self-awareness now becomes an adventure into a world that leads us to challenge what popular belief tells us is 'real'. It is here that we discover what the Fox so wisely understood in Antoine de Saint-Exupéry's *The Little Prince*: 'It is only with the heart that one can see rightly; what is essential is invisible to the eye.'

Love Is . . .

Love is the most transformative force known to humankind, and the search to understand its meaning has been the work of philosophers, psychologists and poets throughout the ages. William Wordsworth tells us: 'Of magic so potent over sun and stars is love.'

There are many definitions of love, and each can be linked to some combination of the four levels of existence, mental, physical, emotional and spiritual. As we seek a deeper understanding of leadership, and open to higher states of being, the energy of the heart invites us to embrace unconditional love in order to become more integrated. As the soul takes authority over our direction, the ego's definitions no longer dominate our decision-making process, but provide a valuable contribution to our ongoing spiritual unfolding and psychological well-being.

Without self-love, it is hard to grow. Most of us are our own worst enemies, criticising and punishing ourselves for being less than perfect. We adopt patterns of self-criticism, failing to acknowledge our strengths and positive qualities, and as a result we get stuck. If we don't respect ourselves, it is hard to love others.

There is no research suggesting that we become more effective by dwelling on what is wrong with us, and then beating up on ourselves. It's important to learn from our mistakes and the errors of our ways so we don't repeat the same situations. However, forgiveness and self-acceptance are essential to our ongoing development. If we are to go on growing, we have to be open to a process of continuous learning, letting go of the guilt, the fear and the shame that keep us from loving ourselves.

Love challenges us in ways that no other energy can, causing us to open ourselves to the most profound experiences of joy and sorrow in the quest for fulfilment of our soul's intention. Kahlil Gibran in *The Prophet* describes it this way:

When love beckons to you, follow him,
Though his ways are hard and steep.
And when his wings enfold you yield to him,
Though the sword hidden in his pinions may wound you . . .
For even as love crowns you so shall he crucify you.
Even as he is for your growth, so he is for your pruning.
Even as he ascends to your height and
Caresses your tenderest branches that quiver in the sun,
So shall he descend to your roots and shake them in their clinging
to the earth . . .
All these things shall love do unto you that you may know
the secrets of your heart
And in that knowledge become a fragment of Life's heart.

Opening the Heart

The Fourth Key prompts us to explore the *relationship with our essence*, in other words the essential self, or that which is connected to a Supreme Being. Given a thousand names, including 'God' and 'Great Spirit', this higher Source of energy is believed to coalesce in the human heart. It is the power of this centre that illuminates our path and invites us to make a commitment to be true to ourselves in the service of others. Here we are asked to relinquish all past understanding of love and look deep within to find Love's meaning.

To love unconditionally is an act of courage, and one that requires an extraordinary commitment to our own awakening. When we open our heart to love we are opening the door to all our hopes and fears, our dreams and desires, our secrets and our sorrows. This source of our deeper authority is not something that we can find outside ourselves, but rather an expression of who we already are, waiting to be expressed in its fullness.

We have to be willing to face the shadow side of our nature if we are to take responsibility for leadership. We have to empty out all the dark emotions, such as guilt, envy, greed, sorrow, revenge, jealousy, anger and hatred, that we have harboured to justify keeping love out. It's a risk that many of us are not yet willing to take in our materialistic and rationally biased society.

However, people who have taken this risk, and who are open-hearted, are characterised by a generosity of spirit. They give freely of themselves in the way that they live their lives. They are excellent listeners and are able to offer a safe space in which others feel heard, so as to allow them to discover the voice of their soul's authority. These people are full of empathy and create opportunities for us to reveal our vulnerabilities and face our fears. They are an inspiration to others.

We often hold ourselves back from trusting enough to love, because of our earliest experiences of betrayal by an important person in our lives. It could be a mother, father, sister, brother or some other person whom we believed loved us unconditionally. The more experiences of this nature we encounter through life, the higher the walls we build. Rather than risk any further pain we shut others out and ourselves in, and the *fear of betrayal* prevents us from taking the risks necessary to fully open our hearts to love. Fear, by its very nature, not only contracts the muscles in our heart, it also leads us to withdraw from making our full contribution and experiencing the fullness of life.

Fear held in the heart restricts the flow of energy needed to build healthy and loving relationships with others. It shuts out the light. When we are afraid to make the changes and take the risks necessary to love fully, we close our hearts. Instead of really living, fear moves us into an existence of 'half-heartedness' and compromise.

It is no surprise that if we do allow fear to dominate our hearts, we are likely to feel a pain or tightening in our chest. Unfortunately, we then compound the situation by making lifestyle choices that increase the risks to our health. Failing to open our hearts can lead to a lonely and 'hard-hearted' existence.

When we make the commitment to reconnect with our soul's authority we sometimes find ourselves shedding light on old wounds that need to be healed before we can claim our full leadership potential. In doing this work we continue the process of becoming a whole person. We find the forgiveness we need, for ourselves and for others, and free the energy to love unconditionally. If we do not heal these old wounds, they will unconsciously govern our lives. They cause us to demand more and more from others in an attempt to satisfy our own needs, holding us back from experiencing deeper levels of intimacy and preventing us owning our authentic power. It takes courage and commitment to push through some of this tough stuff and a willingness to reach out for support.

Some of us, when venturing into this process, can over-identify with our wound or wounds. When we indulge it for too long, our woundedness takes over our lives, stopping us from growing. If we continue to blame our parents, our partners, our friends or anyone else who betrayed us, and never find the forgiveness we need to be whole again, we get stuck in focusing outward and wasting energy. Once we get to the source of our pain it is important not to continue to deepen it ourselves. We have to find the courage and compassion we need to let it go.

Henri J. M. Nouwen says in his beautiful book, *The Inner Voice of Love*, 'There is a deep hole in your being, like an abyss. You will never succeed in filling that hole, because your needs are inexhaustible. You have to work around it so it gradually closes. Since the hole is so enormous and your anguish so deep, you will always be tempted to flee from it. There are two extremes to avoid: being completely absorbed in your pain or being so distracted by so many things that you stay far away from the wound you want to heal.'

The Value of Compassion

Essential to claiming authentic leadership is the spiritual value of compassion. We need to be deeply compassionate with ourselves and with others if we are to express our full potency. Like love, compassion results from discovering the true meaning of forgiveness. To forgive is an act of grace, one that allows us to recognise our own and others' fallibility. Compassion allows us to release old resentments and break free from the past. Holding on to old wounds does not usually affect the people who hurt us, it only prevents us from accessing our authentic power.

Roger Walsh reminds us that 'forgiving does not mean condoning harmful behaviour. Forgiveness is a relinquishment of one's resentment, not a relinquishment of one's ethics.' Once we have found the compassion to forgive, we release the ill feelings that we have harboured and begin to feel grateful for the learning that has come from the pain.

Intimacy and Healing

To help us in the process of uncovering our heart's deeper knowing, many of us enter into a form of 'sacred partnership'. This could be with a life companion, a mentor, a close friend or relative, a spiritual teacher or anyone in whom we truly trust. We have to risk allowing them to see behind the walls that we have erected to protect ourselves. These walls, if strong enough, can shut in our authentic Self, ultimately preventing us from the very thing most of us long for – to give love and be loved in return.

Sometimes, when we think of the energy of the heart, we think of two people coming together in a committed relationship to support each other's unique path to wholeness. To journey with a soul mate, and to share life together for as long as we are able to serve our own and each other's spiritual growth, is perhaps one of the greatest privileges we can know. Such companionship is what many of us seek, and those who are blessed to find it know only too well how precious it is. These are not relationships of romantic love, although they may begin this way, they are relationships that challenge us to break down the walls and reveal the truth of who we are.

To trust someone enough to begin dismantling the very protection that has kept us safe for years requires a commitment to ourselves to relinquish all attachment to the past, and to learn to live fully in the present. These relationships are a great blessing because they allow us to discharge the hurts and hardships that we have held on to, and that can hold us back from accessing our true leadership potential. Sometimes the intensity of such connections can be as excruciating as they are liberating. They challenge us in ways that are hard to imagine.

> Gordon was in his early forties when he met Cathy. They were working in the same company, although they were in different departments. He was in the process of separating and she was divorced. When they first saw each other at a meeting they both had a strong desire to discover more about each other and so found a way of sitting together at lunch. They described how the rest of the world seemed to disappear as they engaged in conversation. Neither of them ate very much and they admitted feeling a bit like teenagers.
>
> They began seeing each other outside the office and felt like they were being drawn together by some invisible force. It wasn't all a bed of roses. Each one was pushing the other's buttons in ways that no one had ever done before, but their love and respect for each other was like nothing they had ever experienced in any previous relationship. It wasn't always easy to be together and they both had to face some stuff within themselves that they would rather have kept buried.
>
> As time went on, the company decided to move Cathy

> to another country. It was a significant career step for her and Gordon did not want to get in the way. At the same time it was extremely confronting to him and he had to make some very tough choices. He described how he felt torn in two – he loved Cathy deeply and yet his ego was hard to pacify. After much soul-searching he knew there was only one real choice and that was to follow his heart. For him, life without Cathy would have been in some way meaningless – she had opened him up to a new understanding of love. He now saw this as the ultimate test of his commitment to his search for a deeper truth. It was a major turning point. He knew that his own future success and fulfilment would be limited without the rich spiritual companionship that they shared.

Relationships of this kind, where we find a perfect mirror to help us rediscover our inner realities, take us to the depths and heights of love's ecstasy. They can lead people to leave their homes, families and past ways of life behind them. There are thousands of books filled with stories of the power of this love and the extraordinary lengths to which people will go to fulfil it.

These relationships are of a very different quality than those that we find when we explore the energy of the Second Key, because they lead us beyond physical intimacy into higher realms. Even the sexual connection in such partnerships is transformed into a spiritual experience. For it is not simply the passion of attraction and the desire to resolve the sense of duality and separation that draws these people together, it is the hearts' desire for a union with a deeper source of Love. It is a love that can only be found when we recognise that it lives deep within each of us.

If we continue to believe that love lies outside ourselves, we are likely to confuse desire with attachment. It is then that the objects of our affections can become an obsession and lead us to become a prisoner of love. Constantly afraid of losing our lover, we crave their attention, never feeling whole without them, and ironically never feeling satisfied for more than short periods of time, when we're with them. For if we confuse 'need' with 'love' we are unlikely to experience our authentic power and achieve this exquisite union.

It is not uncommon for people to use the phrase 'I love you' to mean 'I need you'. Without knowing how to love another unconditionally, we continue to 'love' our partners for as long as that person is able to satisfy our needs. If they fail to, and they always will, the result inevitably will be pain and sorrow. Roger Walsh describes this as 'false love', and says, 'This is a recipe for disaster. Another lover, another spouse, another adoring crowd may offer temporary satisfaction. Yet as long as the inner fears and insecurities remain unrecognised and unhealed, outside rewards bring temporary relief at best.'

In Buddhism, the second of the Four Noble Truths tells us that the cause of all suffering is attachment. When we are attached to something, be it a person or an object, then it is unlikely that we will know love's deeper truth or the power that comes from a heart that is liberated. Freeing ourselves from the fears and insecurities that drive us to create 'false love' is by no means a simple task.

When we find someone or something to fill a void within ourselves, then whatever it is we use as a substitute becomes the object of our attachment. If the attachment results from an absence of self-love, which is normally the case, then letting go takes a great deal of discipline and a very clear intention to find the love that lies within. In our attempt to fill the gap created by an absence of self-love, we sometimes over-give to others at home and at work. This is not self-love but self-sacrifice and it leaves us empty and demanding, in ways that others can never satisfy.

Inviting Support

We often need outside support as we start cutting the cords of attachment and reclaim our soul's authority. Divorce is not uncommon when we touch the deeper energies of the heart and reconnect to our authentic self. At these times we are likely to confront some strong emotions, like anger and grief, before we rediscover the love, and the generosity of the spirit, that is our birthright. Friends are invaluable at times like this to hold us as we struggle through the confusion that accompanies any breakthrough to a new level of awareness.

The sense of liberation and deep inner security that accompanies such a release takes us to higher states of consciousness and opens our hearts to being more accepting and compassionate of ourselves and others. For many of us, feelings of the heart are uncharted territory and a strong support network can be like a 'safety net' when we find ourselves between trapezes with no idea what lies on the other side.

Many of us stop ourselves from living simply by holding on to what has gone before and fearing what may lie ahead. If we want access to our soul's authority then we must be willing to release attachment to both the past and the future. Frances Vaughan, psychologist and author of *Shadows of the Sacred*, says, 'Fear is about the future and guilt about the past – Love lives in present time.' Yet there is so much to distract us from the here and now that it takes a great deal of awareness to remain in the moment. One of the finest supports for bringing our awareness into the present is to focus on our breathing. This fourth energy centre is located near the heart and the lungs, and interestingly, in French '*inspiré*' means 'to breathe in'.

Unconditional love is the driving force that unlocks the energy of the Fourth Key. To know it, we must learn forgiveness and compassion so our hearts can open to the potential for leadership that lies within each of us. Love, according to the wisdom of ages, is the very purpose of the human experience. Once we accept ourselves unconditionally, then we are ready to make healthy choices that allow us to contribute to the lives of others. We are able to let go of the fear-based choices that we rationalise as being in others' and our own best interests, but which in our hearts we know keep us in situations that prevent us from growing. When Love is in the driver's seat, we see through very different eyes that transform our consciousness and the very purpose and meaning of leadership.

Key Questions

- What brings you joy?
- When does your head get in the way of your heart?
- Are you compassionate enough with yourself and others? Who do you need to forgive?
- When do you feel the Love in your heart?
- How much of your time do you spend thinking about the past and/or the future?
- What are you grateful for in this moment?
- How might the 'fear of betrayal' hold you back?

Organisational Implications

It's always a risky business to talk about love, especially in the context of business and leadership. Today, it is becoming more of a topic of conversation in organisations that are seeking to achieve higher levels of service and customer excellence. It doesn't take a genius to know that control and fear create restrictions and inhibit people from producing excellent results. Therefore, it is only common sense to recognise that an environment that is more acknowledging of the human spirit, and people's need to be respected, yields higher levels of productivity. So how do we go about putting the 'L' back in leadership in an organisational context?

Most Western people spend more of their waking hours at their places of work than they do at home. So it is vital to create a climate that is more supportive of our fundamental human natures. Qualities such as generosity, compassion, wisdom, gratitude and respect need to be cultivated if organisations are to foster the authentic leadership power needed to be effective in this age when more importance is being placed on relationships.

It is naive today to assume people will perform simply because they are being paid a wage or a salary. We all know that it is not extrinsic rewards that motivate people, but rather the intrinsic motivation that people gain from feeling good about themselves and their contributions. And yet there are those who still describe all of this 'soft stuff' as optional extras!

The issue here has more to do with having the knowledge and competency necessary to navigate the field of these subtle energies, rather than an absence of valuing the spiritual and emotional side of the equation. The Seven Keys are designed specifically to help bridge this gap and provide insights and guidance into these 'invisible', yet profound, influences that impact organisational life.

Awakening the Heart

The energy released by the Fourth Key opens the door to the deeper dimensions of leadership by inspiring the heart in the context of work. Kahlil Gibran suggests that 'work is love made visible'.

> Ken Bertaccini, a former president of the Consumer Products Division of AT&T, was an early pioneer in the area of inspirational leadership. He worked with his team to create a pyramid of values, which had 'Love' at its core. He admitted at the time that: 'Using love in this context is a bold step, but I think we're ready to legitimise the 'L' word and put love in our business . . . We're talking about love in the context of love your neighbour as you love yourself, and treat others as you would like to be treated. We don't hold with the scenario that there's no room for love in business. We all need to love one another to exist individually or collectively whether it's on a personal level or a business level. Adding love to our Shared Values challenges us to live our personal values of trust and respect . . . Certainly these are all definitions of love.'

In carrying out a survey for a client organisation in Europe, I was amazed at the number of people in leadership roles who talked about love. I asked one manager what he thought was the most important quality of an effective leader. To my surprise he replied: 'To love your people, to take time to listen to them so that they feel seen and understood – if you don't do this you will never get their trust.'

The author of *The Seven Habits of Highly Effective People*, Stephen Covey, explores 'Living the Law of Love' in his book *Principle-Centered Leadership*: 'We encourage obedience to the Laws of Life when we live the Laws of Love. People are extremely tender inside, particularly those who act as if they are tough and self-sufficient. And if we'll listen to them with the third ear, the heart, they'll tell us so. We can gain greater influence with them by showing love, particularly unconditional love, as this gives people a sense of intrinsic worth and security, unrelated to conforming behaviour or comparisons with others.'

A colleague working with a team of managers asked them what they wanted in order to perform at higher levels of effectiveness. Their reply, as is often the case, was: 'We want more fun!' Not satisfied with his understanding of exactly what they meant, he asked them to describe what having more fun would look like. To his amazement their answer was simply: 'To really love our work'.

The corporate consultant and writer Kymn Harvin Rutigliano says: 'Love is the heart of service. Observe those who truly model excellent customer service and they will epitomise two things: loving what they do and loving people – people who they serve. They might never say the "L" word but there is that sense about them. And this "sense" adds up to big dollars and cents, competitive advantage, customer loyalty, high employee morale – in short, business success.'

In most cases it is not just what we do, but the attitudes and perspectives that we take to our work. When we are respected, respect ourselves and respect others, we will feel we're adding value, as this little story illustrates. A woman whose task was to place pension cheques in envelopes (what might appear as a rather mundane and repetitive task to many) was asked why she was always so happy at work. Her reply was inspiring: 'I provide the means by which the elderly in our society can grow old with dignity.' Instead of looking at the activity itself, she saw her job as something that added considerable value to the lives of those she felt she was serving. The desire to add value and make a contribution is part of the foundation of the alliance mindset. It means shifting from a predominant focus on 'what's in it for me' to one where there is a wish to be of service to others.

> A team of IT specialists had got feedback that they were failing to meet their internal customers' needs. It was tough to receive because they thought they were doing the best they could under the circumstances. The team leader took the comments to heart and decided to engage in a twelve-month process to transform the department's approach. Prior to this time many of the members operated as individual contributors and knew very little about one another, preferring to focus on their own area of expertise. This was a huge part of the problem because the customer always got a different answer depending on who they happened to talk to on any given day.
>
> After gathering more data from the customer population to enable a deeper look at the issues, the IT folks engaged in a series of meetings with different components. Some of the meetings involved just themselves, and others engaged them in dialogue with their customers. The results surprised everybody. At the first meeting the after-dinner conversation was all about work. At the second meeting it was more about story and joke-telling. After the third it was like the best kind of family gathering – they played games, laughed and had fun and really found they were getting closer to each other. One of the sessions had involved some outdoor activity in which two of the members took considerable personal risks to save a third. It brought them very close together as a team.
>
> Back at work, the IT department's productivity and the customer satisfaction indexes showed a marked increase. They received comments like 'I feel I'm talking to a real human being who understands me and doesn't make me think I'm technologically illiterate' and 'At last I have

> somewhere to go when I want to find out what these machines can really do to help my business.' All the members credited their leader for having the insight to bring them together in order to break down the walls that kept them intellectually and emotionally separate from each other. They felt he had 'served them well' and as a result everyone benefited.

Robert Greenleaf, creator of the concept of Servant-Leadership, has always maintained that 'the servant leader is servant first. It begins with the natural feeling that one wants to serve. Then conscious choice brings one to aspire to lead.' It seems that love, leadership and service fit together nicely, and that cultivating such an orientation is of considerable value to all stakeholders.

Networks and Learning Partnerships

The Fourth Key has a lot to do with building productive networks and partnerships, whether it is with customers, suppliers, employees or managers. Developing close one-on-one relationships requires a different set of skills than managing a business. It has more to do with trust and empathy, and less to do with technical and managerial competence. When people come together in learning partnerships their task ability is usually a given and it is their potential to be open and authentic in close relationships that becomes a critical factor for success.

For partnerships to be successful in the business arena each individual needs to have a very clear identity and secure personal boundaries. They need to be willing to join together to create a shared purpose, which serves them individually and as a twosome. In a true learning partnership neither sacrifices their individuality but they connect in ways that enrich their own and their partner's soul's intention and does something that they could not do alone. There is no sense of co-dependency as there is with a one-up, one-down relationship found in the compliance mindset, just a strong sense of interconnection and mutual trust.

Developing a 'social contract' that defines the relationship process of their agreement is a very important step in forming a partnership and one that is overlooked all too often in the organisational context. For this to be effective it needs to contain the following:

- A clear statement of purpose
- Clarification on power and decision-making
- How to handle disagreements
- Frequency and nature of interaction
- Relationship reviews
- Third-party intervention
- Termination of partnership

This last point is one of the most critical. The tough part is recognising when a partnership is over and being able to move apart with dignity and gratitude. Many people stay together long past the sell-by date of the relationship! Their shared purpose has been fulfilled (or is not going to be fulfilled) and the partnership no longer serves the individuals. Somewhere there is an assumption that 'if partnerships are good they should never end'. It's an assumption that needs to be challenged over and over again until we understand the true nature of interdependence – relationships end and it's OK. There is no failure in this. The failure comes when we don't recognise it has ended and hold on beyond that time when the purpose of the partnership has been served.

Operating in global networks is different from working within a national hierarchy, and requires a whole new set of leadership competencies. These include working with material and spiritual values, integration of the past and the future into the present, compassion for all stakeholders and their points of view and the willingness to serve the good of the whole. Openness to learning coupled with unconditional positive regard promotes the high-performance work cultures in which people feel free to access their leadership capabilities. Organisations that are truly committed to being global are focusing their energy on creating productive networks with processes that reward and encourage such attributes in the service of their overall missions.

The concept of 'celebration' is also something that is commanding more attention as recognition grows that happiness, health and productivity go hand in hand. Those in leadership roles who support an orientation to celebration get a high yield on their investment. All of this is clearly common sense, but with so much inertia, and a focus that is predominantly short-term, it is a formidable challenge to open the space for these leadership qualities to emerge – even though few would argue against their importance in achieving concrete results.

The following are the leadership skills and capabilities of the Fourth Key.

Leadership Capabilities

- Lives in present time
- Enjoys life
- Balances the head and the heart
- Respects the dignity of others
- Sees and acknowledges the good in everyone
- Celebrates success
- Engages with compassion and empathy
- Creates learning partnerships

Global Implications

Everything we see around us in the world today is the product of our collective consciousness. We are all contributing to the ongoing process of this creation we describe as reality. We may not be doing it with conscious intent but nevertheless we are each an influential part of this vast network of humanity that spans the globe. Every thought we hold, everything we do has a consequence on the vitality of the whole. If we are fearful then we will manifest fear. If we are loving we will manifest love – it's that simple.

Unconditional Love

Moving from a fear-based orientation to a place of unconditional love and compassion is not easy; it takes tremendous courage and commitment. As Gandhi reminded us: 'We each must be the change we want to see in the world.' Love begins at home in our own hearts, and then radiates outwards. But love is by no means passive. It is active – it is visible in our behaviour and in our attitudes towards others. Every second we're alive we are either choosing (consciously or otherwise) to promote kindness, generosity, gratitude and caring or we are choosing not to.

The Dalai Lama tells us: 'genuine compassion is based on a clear acceptance or recognition that others, like oneself, want happiness and have the right to overcome suffering.' He believes that happiness is our birthright and that love is the source of liberation from pain. This message has been consistent throughout the ages. Philosophers, mystics, sages, holy women and men and the great prophets all tell us the same thing: that we are the ones who can eliminate war and suffering, and bring peace to Earth. It is not someone else; it's in every one of us. This is the function of leadership in a global society; to inspire unconditional love and to promote the abundance and sharing that comes from hearts that are open and free from suffering.

Research funded by the Institute of Noetic Sciences into the effects of altruism has established a solid database to support the premise that by doing good to others we strengthen ourselves. By giving of ourselves unconditionally, we receive the riches of spirit that keep us healthy. When we care for others and are cared for in return, we enjoy better physical and psychological well-being individually and collectively.

The transformation of consciousness is well underway in the world today. People are waking up to the realisation that we are the authors, the producers and the directors. We are the ones who are being held accountable for manifesting the divine plan here on Earth. It is not somebody else who is responsible for the results we are getting – it's you and me!

This expansion of our awareness that 'all is one' is blowing minds wide open as individuals within their disciplines begin to realise that the boundaries of separation are illusory if viewed from higher ground. Edgar Mitchell, one of the early US astronauts, had such an experience when he looked down from the moon at his home planet and saw that there were 'no dotted lines between the countries'.

As we venture into a new century, it will be the energy of the heart that awakens us to this realisation. All the spiritual traditions believe this to be so, and it is only in the interpretations of certain religious dogma that love is lost in the quest for power and domination. To my knowledge, none of the truly great spiritual leaders have ever decreed death and destruction as a path to salvation.

Jean Houston, in a paper written for the World Business Academy's quarterly journal *Perspectives* (December 1998), said: 'Through it all, beneath it all creating and sustaining it all is the presence of Love. Love that is tender and raging, always yearning and utterly complete. Love that burns in our marrow, draws us into mystery, forgives our unskilled behaviour, calls us into greatness.' This is the source of our true leadership potency.

VOICING TRUTH

Once lit, the flame of truth will never go out.
Plato

THE FIFTH KEY

Characteristics
Unlocked
Honest, authentic, integrated, self-expressive, aligned, innovative, attuned, committed, quality listener
Locked
Withholding, emotionally inexpressive, guarded, untruthful, self-doubting, flippant, superficial, double-talker, unclear of personal beliefs, cynical

Personal Implications

THE FIFTH OF THE LEADERSHIP Keys supports us in bringing together the heart and the head through the act of communication. Physically, the neck and the throat connect the head to the rest of the body and act as a bridge between them. We sometimes say we are 'choked up' or have got things 'stuck in our throats', when we seek to express difficult emotions in ways that will be understood. Alternatively, there are certain things that we 'find hard to swallow' when we are faced with something that either confronts us, or doesn't sound like the truth. This centre also influences the ears and is linked to the energies of sound and vibration.

Unlocking our full leadership potential means accessing the energy of self-expression, allowing us the freedom to share our thoughts and our feelings through authentic communication. It is one thing to say what we think others want to hear, and quite another to state the truth about what we deeply believe. When we do, we become vulnerable, disclosing what's important to us and revealing a little more of what makes us tick. It is the *fear of humiliation* that holds people back from speaking in these ways and is one of the reasons public speaking drives 'terror' into the hearts of millions!

Most of us have ego-driven personalities that we have developed to allow us to achieve success in the material world. We know just what to do and what to say in order to look good and be accepted. When we are conscious of being on a spiritual path, and look inward for the answers to life's questions, the story changes. Once we become more aware of our own deeper values and beliefs, we no longer feel comfortable simply toeing the party line. As we learn to listen to the voice of our soul's authority, we are less willing to tolerate the incongruities that exist between what is said and what is done. As a result our whole orientation to leadership changes.

The throat centre is sometimes referred to as 'the gateway to higher consciousness' because in the Western system of understanding the chakras, it is the first of the three vortices that relate directly to spiritual energy. It is the point at which we transition from having infinite choice to accepting that ultimately there is only one choice that has any real meaning.

When we are under the influence of the compliance mindset, we follow the 'shoulds' of life, feeling like we have no choice other than to buy into the patterns of our families or social groups. After awakening to the energy of the Second and Third Keys we find we have as many choices as we want, and can assert ourselves and determine our own path through life. By the time we turn the Fourth Key, we are already becoming aware of a divine presence in our lives and begin to focus our attention inward, more of the time.

By unlocking the Fifth Key we begin the process of listening more consciously to the voice of our soul's authority. We become increasingly aware of a part of ourselves that we intuitively know expresses the truth of who we are in terms of our God-given heritage. This inner wisdom provides us the guidance we need to follow. It helps us to free our attachment to struggle, and leads us to a place of ongoing learning and enlightenment. We wake up to the ultimate choice, to follow Divine Will and claim our authentic leadership power – or not.

Voices in our Head

Many of us are unable to hear the voice of our deeper truth because of the constant chatter that so often clutters our minds and keeps us distracted. In our activity-driven society, we are told that if we are not busy we are being lazy or at the very least unproductive. We have a thousand voices inside our heads trying to get our attention and take our focus away from the wisdom inside us. Some of these voices are rooted in deep-seated fears that have been around forever. Others are just the familiar voices that have been telling us how, and who, we should be if we really want to achieve and 'be someone'.

Hal and Sidra Stone describe in their book *Embracing Our Selves* how we have a number of different sub-personalities that are vying to get our attention. They have given names to these voices: the inner critic, the protector/controller, the victim, the perfectionist, the caretaker, the pusher, the good mother/father, the rebellious son/daughter and the vulnerable child, to name but a few.

Sometimes it is the inner critic that speaks loudest and tells us we're too fat, too weak, too slow, too soft, too hard or too lazy. Other times it might be the perfectionist, who is always driving us to be perfect (something we will never achieve). Whenever one of these 'selves' takes charge we are likely to be out of balance in our communication.

A lot of this happens unconsciously, and we are unaware that we are under the influence of these sub-personalities – a condition that some of them would like to maintain! However, once we are in touch with the voice of our soul's authority we begin the process of consciously taking back control from the myriad of energy patterns that have been running our lives. The objective here is not to negate or destroy these energies, but rather to ensure that it is our true Self, and not a sub-personality, that is our principal guide through life.

Once we make the commitment to reconnect with our spiritual

nature we can actively explore the *relationship with our Higher Self.* Such an investigation requires discipline if we are to take charge of the random wanderings of our meandering minds, and quiet the incessant noise in our heads. Anyone who has ever attempted to meditate knows exactly how hard it is to let go of all the thoughts that are constantly seeking to get our attention. Only by practice can we free ourselves from the ego's energy patterns that keep us in what John Scherer refers to as our 'adaptive routines'. These are sets of behaviours that mask our soul's expression and allow our ego and its fears to run our lives.

Truth and Freedom

One of the greatest challenges of this Key is being willing to tell ourselves the truth about what we think, how we feel and the quality of our life. Many people are very comfortable with maintaining the status quo, and look upon spiritual seekers as lost and lonely souls. They tell themselves that they're happy to make the compromises that have to be made, in order to avoid making changes. They remain in relationships and jobs that are less than satisfying because they don't want to rock the boat.

When they look a little deeper, they find that it is not contentment that keeps them where they are, but an underlying fear. Unknowingly, it is often the fear of transformation that keeps people stuck in situations they 'know' aren't right for them. They're afraid of what might happen if they begin living in alignment with a higher truth and an intangible 'something' that they find difficult to articulate.

Voicing the truth about the daily choices we are making is an important step in getting to know ourselves, and living ethically. Becoming authentic in our expression does not necessarily require making dramatic changes to our lives, it may simply mean shifting our perception of reality within our current context. The difference is that once we tell ourselves the truth, we become more conscious of the impact of our choices.

'The truth will set you free' is a statement that has echoed through the ages. It allows us to remove the glasses of self-deception that keep us caught in patterns of lies and deceit, and to choose a more fulfilling path. By doing so we not only deepen our level of self-respect, we also increase the respect we have for others. There are times when we don't tell people the truth because we tell ourselves that 'it's best for them', or that we 'don't want to hurt them'. In some cases this may hold a grain of truth, but more often than not we lie in order to protect ourselves from the consequences of our choices.

When we are honest with our Self, then we are less afraid to be honest with others. This in no way means that we should go around telling people exactly what we think about them, without sensitivity to their feelings! Rather, it means that when we find ourselves holding back the truth, or lying for some reason, we take a careful look at why we are choosing to do so. It is important to look at the possible longer-term consequences of these behaviours on our health and our relationships, resulting from the absence of trust and authenticity.

Telling a New Story

One of the most powerful means we have for personal transformation is by changing the stories we tell to, and about, ourselves. When we learn to listen deeply to a new truth, many of the stories we repeat about who we are, and who we are not, no longer ring true. We shape ourselves and maintain our ego identities through what we say about ourselves. The beliefs we constantly reinforce by telling our stories mould us and keep us as we are, until we consciously choose to change them.

In a meeting recently someone was sharing an event that had happened some years ago. It had been a significant experience for her, and was causing her to hold on to a lot of guilt that was affecting her energy levels and vitality for life. It was clearly not the first time she had shared the story with a group of people. Someone asked her if there was anything new that she had learned from repeating the story – to which she replied, 'No, it's all too familiar.' She was then asked why she was choosing to hold on to the story and what would happen if she let it go.

It triggered a powerful insight for her and she saw very clearly that there was no longer any value in repeating it. After recognising this to be so later that day, she remarked how different she felt, a difference that could be seen physically in her facial expression and her posture.

Our stories literally shape and define us. Sometimes they help us to free ourselves from the past, other times they severely limit our growth. In this case, her story was blocking her true expression and holding her back from taking authentic leadership. For many of us, our personal myths need some re-examination – especially those that limit our growth.

Risks and Rewards

Living without secrets and being conscious of our personal myths allows us to experience increased levels of self-confidence as we express ourselves without fear of what others might think. It means we can make stronger connections with people, and form authentic relationships based on open and honest communication. Such connections provide the opportunity for deeper intimacy and insight. However, being truthful is full of risks:

- We risk being loved for who we are
- We risk being rejected for who we are
- We risk being seen for who we are
- We risk being misunderstood for who we are
- We risk being respected for who we are
- We risk being judged for who we are

Needless to say, the risks of not being truthful to our authentic leadership power are far higher. We risk being 'found out' and losing credibility, and we risk losing ourselves in the lies and the secrets. Those who have done this know only too well the price they have had to pay for failing to be honest with themselves and others. The long-term consequences of living dishonestly can be emotionally and physically costly. Once we have made the choice to be authentic, we start to see the broader consequences of such actions, and are no longer able to tolerate such behaviour within ourselves.

We then have to disengage from the behaviours, resolve the emotional aftermath and find compassion for ourselves. By voicing the truth, if only to ourselves, of what we did and how we feel, we will inevitably learn, deepen our spiritual understanding of life and find a new kind of peace.

Tom had been married for fifteen years and had achieved a good deal of professional success. He was a senior executive of a large engineering firm and was regarded as a 'bold clear leader'. He loved his work and found it challenging and rewarding. He was very much an extrovert and enjoyed involving people in solving problems and making decisions. He was well liked by almost everyone and although he sometimes got a little heavy-handed people respected his leadership.

At home Tom had three children, to whom he was a devoted father. His marriage had, from his perspective, not been ideal for some years, but rather than talking things over with his wife he found himself engaging in an affair. At first it was easy for him to keep his worlds separate. 'I was able to see things in different compartments and as long as I could keep it that way, I could justify my behaviour.'

In time, Tom's wife became suspicious and confronted him with the evidence she had found of his other relationship. He decided to lie rather than to come clean. He didn't want to hurt his wife and break up the family. He later realised that there was another reason that led him to cover it up – he didn't want to suffer the humiliation that he thought would result from the truth.

So instead of facing the consequences of his choices, Tom continued strengthening his other relationship and dug himself deeper into the lie he was living. It wasn't long before everything erupted and he began to see how he had created two lives. His strong sense of responsibility was keeping him in his marriage while his heart was drawing him deeper into a relationship that was helping him to grow. By now he couldn't keep things compartmentalised, his personal world was a mess and it was having a significant impact on his leadership effectiveness. His inner critic was having a wonderful time telling him how terrible he was, and soon Tom became consumed by guilt and shame.

He tried to bury himself in work but there was no escape. He felt lousy and insecure. He lost all sense of his power and found it hard to function in any area of his life. The torment was intense as he was torn between his deep sense of responsibility as a father for keeping his family together, and his desire to engage in a fulfilling partnership with his loving companion. At some level he knew that the real issue was deeper than simply making a choice between the two women but he was scared.

He couldn't continue maintaining the split between his head and his heart and knew that he had to make finding his own truth the priority. 'I knew that there was no easy answer and so I made the declaration to myself to become a person of integrity that I could respect. At the time I had no attachment to a specific outcome, I just knew that making a commitment to living true to myself was the first step in a process of becoming whole. I was hurting too many people through my own self-deception.'

The Value of Integrity

Integrity is the spiritual value associated with the Fifth Key. It is the integration of our mind, body, spirit and emotions in the expression of who we are, in alignment with our soul's intention. In other words, living in ways that are congruent with our higher values and what we hold to be true. When we are living with integrity, we feel at ease with ourselves and we feel 'integrated'. Such experiences of wholeness create fulfilment and satisfaction leading to feelings of well-being. An absence of truth, on the other hand, promotes stress and illnesses, especially at the throat-centre, including ear and throat infections, and chronic dry coughs.

Integrating the head and the heart through honest communication is an essential learning associated with this Key and critical to expressing authentic leadership. Tom's story shows how if we are out of integrity in one area of our life, it will impact on us wherever we are and result in a loss of power. Caroline Myss tells us: 'If head and heart are not communicating clearly with each other, one will dominate the other. When our minds are in the lead we suffer emotionally because we turn emotional data into an enemy. We seek to control all situations and relationships and maintain authority over emotions. When our hearts are in the lead we tend to maintain the illusion that all is well. Whether the mind is in the lead or the heart, "will" is motivated by fear and the futile goal of control, not by a sense of internal security.'

When we learn to listen to the voice of our soul's truth and live in alignment with a higher intention, everything begins to change. The marriage between heart and head creates subtle 'ahas' at first, but day by day they get stronger and clearer and we begin to feel more secure. The quality of both our inner and outer listening improves and we hear things that we didn't pay attention to before. The inner chatter quietens and we are less interested in hearing ourselves repeat the same old stuff we've heard a hundred times before. We become more open to the voices of others. When we do speak, it comes from a different part of ourselves, and we may be surprised at the wisdom of our words!

While the Second Key awakens us to our creative potential, it is the Fifth Key that allows us to begin to manifest our dreams. Words are enormously powerful and people who have found their authentic voice are an inspiration to others. Mark Yeoell talks about the power of 'speaking our vision into reality'. The expression 'as above, so below' relates to the manifestation of divine will through acts of creation. Once we breakthrough the illusion of control, our potential for innovation becomes unlimited. We discover that the more we exercise our creativity, the more our inner light illuminates our path.

Once again, it is the integration of mind, body and spirit through right speech and right action that is constantly being expressed through communication. Whether it is as a result of what we say or what we do (or what we don't say or don't do), we are always communicating. As human beings we cannot 'not communicate'! The more we trust the voice of our innate wisdom, the more authentic our communication will be.

Our authentic leadership comes from finding out who we are, forgiving ourselves for being who we are not and loving ourselves in spite of it all! To reach this place means deeply listening to the still quiet voice within, which provides the guidance that we need to release any outdated patterns of communication. It means choosing to live ethically, trusting our soul's authority and surrendering to the spiritual energy reflective of divine will. It is only through constant communication with our higher Self that we can be freed from relentlessly searching in the outside world, for meaning and satisfaction – a search that can only leave us groping around in the dark feeling empty and disillusioned.

Key Questions

- What is truth?
- When do you say what you really mean? What are the consequences when you don't?
- What are the secrets that stop you from being free?
- How might some of the stories you tell keep you from growing?
- Do you take enough quiet time to listen to your inner voice? What would happen if you did?
- How might 'fear of humiliation' hold you back?

Organisational Implications

The issues relating to Voicing Truth in organisations are plentiful and a lot of them have to do with the corporate culture. The stories that get told repeatedly about 'the way things get done around here' either support or inhibit genuine communication among the players. From my experience the following are the most common reasons for an absence of 'truth telling' in organisational settings:

1 People have never been taught how to communicate authentically
2 The cultural mindset is predominantly compliant and hierarchical
3 People fear the consequences of telling the truth
4 No time is made for dialogue and open discussion
5 People believe others know what's best
6 There is a bias towards knowing the answers and for quick decision-making
7 People look upward and outward, not inward, for direction
8 Management does not value open-ended questions
9 The story is that 'they shoot the messenger'

In order for people to express their authentic leadership power in organisations, there needs to be a fundamental change in these patterns.

> In one European organisation, the new President put together a team made up of bright high-potential employees who named themselves 'the Challengers'. Their purpose was to provide the management team with feedback and proposals for breaking down the barriers that were blocking effectiveness. Some of the recommendations directly related to the communication patterns that the top leadership themselves had been reinforcing. With a strong commitment to change, the management team gradually adopted new behaviours and attitudes, asking the Challengers to keep them honest throughout the process.
>
> In an American organisation, the CEO created 'mess

teams' made up of a cross-section of the population. Their task was to inform the management team when they 'messed up'. The mess teams then worked together with the management to 'clean up the mess' in ways that promoted greater sharing of accountability throughout the organisation.

These are just two examples of the authentic leadership that is emerging to support greater truth and openness in communication.

Deeper Listening

One of the things that have always surprised me is how much people appreciate learning fundamental life skills, like listening and building effective relationships. So few of those entering organisations, and many at middle and senior management, have ever received basic education in the softer skill areas of communication. The art of conversation and the tools for effective dialogue are not required courses at schools and universities! Without them, the potential for growth of individuals and organisations is seriously limited. With a stronger focus on customers and an emphasis on relationship management, communication skills can lead to competitive advantage in areas where there is little differentiation between product and price.

James Autry says in *The Art of Caring Leadership*: 'Listen. In every office you hear the threads of love and joy and fear and guilt, the cries for celebration and reassurance, and somehow you know that connecting those threads is what you are supposed to do and business takes care of itself.'

One of the basic building blocks for authentic power is the ability to listen. In *Collins' English Dictionary*, 'to listen' is defined as 'to heed or to pay attention'. Listening is perhaps singularly the most critical leadership skill and probably the least developed in most of us who are driven to achieve results. To listen takes time, a desire for connection and, as the definition suggests, attention. When we really listen to someone, we often recognise the similarities between us. We discover that it is only the ego that leads us to focus on our differences and adopt more of a competitive orientation. With so many things to do and so many places to be, it's hard to stay still long enough to listen to anything except the voice of the 'pusher'. This is the all too familiar voice which is constantly driving us to meet our deadlines, and distracts us from what is happening in the here and now.

Listening is an act of respect. When we take the time to listen to someone we acknowledge their existence and they feel valued. Children who are not listened to by their parents will play up just to get attention, reinforcing the adage, 'love me, hate me, but please don't ignore me'. Listening is what builds connection, and strengthens trust and respect in the alliance mindset. Yet it is a competence that is underdeveloped in organisations today, especially where 'speed' is valued above just about everything!

Sarita Chawla, in her work on 'Dialogue', has developed the following 'Five Levels of Listening'.

- *In Your Own World* – not listening at all
- *Judge and Miser* – listening with judgement or withholding
- *Interrupter extraordinaire, I know best* – listening and interrupting while thinking: let me tell you how it really is
- *Genuinely Curious* – listening as though you really want to know
- *Rapt Listening* – listening with an ability to reflect back, with a willingness to be influenced, and remaining fully present

In meetings, it is commonplace to experience the first three levels, with everyone presenting their case, and with little time for genuine exchange of views. New concepts are put forward, judged and dismissed rather than being constructively explored and built upon. In the end people don't want to go to meetings because there is no added value. They feel unable to make worthwhile contributions and would rather just get on with their own 'stuff'.

Learning to listen both inwardly and outwardly is one of the cornerstones to authentic leadership and the prerequisite for Voicing Truth. Many organisations suffer from an affliction called 'political politeness' – disorder where the 'higher-ups' never hear what the 'lower-downs' think about how things really are. Instead, they get a version of the truth that has been predigested, neutered and rehearsed. Organisational reviews become mundane, void of any spice and with very little return on the energy invested.

Operating with Integrity

There are many temptations in organisations that challenge integrity and draw us into the dark side. The news is full of scams and shams. The recent crises of confidence in corporations like Enron and WorldCom have only served to highlight how the drive for self-interest can take second place to the desire to serve the common good. The power of possession and the power of position are seductive forces and can cause people to hide the truth of what they know to be so. The cost of doing so is always high.

Large institutions of all kinds, from governments to corporations, from religious organisations to hospitals, have always been fertile fields for either serving the highest good or falling prey to corruption. Not just in the financial sense. Integrity in institutions has as much to do with living true to a set of principles and values as it does with ensuring the accounting practices are ethical. Sexual harassment, discrimination and child abuse are clearly major breaches in ethics. Whatever lies people tell themselves to make it OK to participate, support or collude in these behaviours, somewhere inside they know they are 'out of integrity'.

It is the more subtle and gradual erosion of truth-telling that is often more difficult to identify than the unlawful practices. Stealing others' ideas and not giving them credit, back-stabbing, doing what the boss says even when we know it is wrong, burying data, thinking one thing and saying another: almost all of us have done some of these – you could say it is part of human nature. The key issue is what we tell ourselves when we engage at this level, whether we are knowingly supporting or encouraging a lack of integrity in organisations, or whether we are simply out of touch with the voice of our deeper authority.

Peter had worked hard preparing the financial forecast for his division. Trying to make the numbers work was difficult and his boss's expectations were high. He'd stretched them as far as he realistically could and knew that it would be a tall order given the limited resources he had available.

Peter's secretary had typed the charts for him to present to the management team and he had gone through them just prior to the meeting. As he presented the forecast he noticed that one of the numbers had been transposed. Instead of reading $329k it read $392k. Unfortunately, Peter didn't have the courage even though he knew it was incorrect to admit the error at the time. His boss was delighted with the forecast and so Peter did not want to disappoint him or to be seen as having not 'proofed' the charts correctly. He felt telling the truth would be costly for his career.

Needless to say his team lost a good deal of respect for him and were unable to meet the 'revised' number. Peter's boss accused him of setting unrealistic targets and being out of touch with the marketplace. He himself was unable to relax for close to twelve months and lived in fear that his 'lie' would catch up with him even though he naively hoped that it wouldn't. It was a mistake that he paid dearly for on many levels.

A Climate of Candour

Paternalistic companies are often 'good news' companies. Nobody wants to upset the leaders and therefore bad news is suppressed. This has a knock-on effect throughout the organisation, from overoptimistic business plans to inaccurate personal assessments to 'flexible accounting practices'.

The focus is on managing upwards, and on second-guessing the boss, to ensure a quiet life. The people in these companies often pride themselves on 'being polite', but store up problems for themselves over time, as Peter found to his cost. In such environments, where the truth does get suppressed, the genius in the organisation remains untapped, and many opportunities for growth are never realised.

Candour creates relationships based on trust rather than on political politeness. Whilst honest relationships can be initially more challenging and time-consuming to build, they are inevitably longer-lasting and more productive. There are still far too few leaders who create a climate of candour and who have the skills to create the opportunity for meaningful conversation. With the pressure growing daily for greater transparency on all levels of organisational functioning, they would do well to invest time in building the needed competencies for authentic communication.

One of the lowest-scoring sections in employee opinion surveys is communications. Much of this has to do with people feeling that they are not heard, and that the truth is kept from them. It is not uncommon to hear people in organisations stating that they don't believe what they're being told, or that management says one thing and does another.

One way paternalistic leaders disempower people is by assuming that they cannot take the truth. By protecting them from the 'way things really are', these well-intentioned managers show disrespect for people's abilities to deal with what's so. The irony is that management loses credibility. Walking the talk has become an important ground rule in many settings, and when people aren't doing so, we know it immediately.

With many organisations engaging in mergers, acquisitions and other significant change processes, it is even more critical for management to be authentic and open with employees. Unfortunately, in the majority of cases, a doctored version of the truth is produced to protect the people, and candid conversation is impossible. Obviously there are certain ethical and business considerations that have to be respected, but in many cases there is far too much 'pussyfooting' around the truth in ways that are not supportive. When the management's attitude is to disrespect people's maturity, then the result is cynicism and apathy – because people know what's really going on.

Candour can lead to higher levels of commitment, especially at times of change. One example of this happened in a corporate forum called a town meeting. The organisation was facing dramatic budget cuts that were guaranteed to change the whole way of working. The vice-president of one of the businesses had called together one hundred of his senior management. After listening to what was described as the company line, someone challenged him to 'tell us how it really is'. After a long pause he put down his notes and began to describe his real views on the coming months.

There was a tangible change in the energy of the group as they heard the truth about their company. People began to ask questions about what they could do and what their options were. They also began to explore some alternatives that hadn't yet been tried. The atmosphere changed from 'Here we go again with the same old stuff' to 'OK, so this is how it really is, what can *we* do?' Needless to say, it was a powerful and uplifting meeting, even though it wasn't good news. It also set the tone for the attitude that was needed to see the company through the tough times that lay ahead, and released a level of cooperation that can only emerge in the face of truth.

Balancing Advocacy and Enquiry

Advocacy is when we share our thoughts and 'speak' our mind: enquiry is when we seek others' thoughts through *genuine* questioning. The traditional styles of management communication reinforce advocacy. The dominance of a 'directive style' of management, with its orientation to telling, is still one of the biggest barriers to people taking leadership responsibility in organisations today. With an increased focus on relationship building, this needs to be balanced with a 'facilitative style', where leaders seek to engage in 'enquiry' with all stakeholders. Probing the views of others and asking questions is a skill that many managers lack, believing they should – or, even worse, that they do – have all the answers! Such beliefs shut out opportunities for learning and leave organisations stuck in ineffective patterns of leadership behaviour.

For many years, we have been coaching leaders to help them increase their style versatility, and broaden their behavioural repertoire. It is very challenging work, especially for those who have been rewarded consistently over a long career for their existing behaviour patterns. What has helped enormously in supporting deeper and more sustainable levels of behaviour change is a move away from the traditional orientation to discussion, and an engagement in a process of genuine dialogue. This does two things. First, it allows people to experience the value of enquiry as a means for personal development, and second, it supports them in practising skills that are more facilitative in nature.

Theoretical physicist David Bohm focused the latter years of his life on the exploration of dialogue, seeing it as a means for changing human consciousness. He differentiated dialogue and discussion by looking at the root of each of the words. 'Dialogue comes from the Greek word *dialogos*. *Logos* means 'the word' or 'the meaning of the word'. And '*dia*' means through – it doesn't mean two . . . The picture or image this derivation suggests is of a stream of meaning flowing among and through us, and between us. Contrast this with 'discussion', which has the same root as 'percussion' and 'concussion'. It really means to break things up.'

When we engage in discussion we interact at the level of opinions, attitudes and behaviours, or what is visible. We are seeking to *influence or convince* others to adopt our point of view. Discussion either reinforces the opinions we already hold or causes us to think again. It often results in win–lose outcomes. When overdone in an organisational setting it inhibits truth-telling and perpetuates the status quo.

When we engage in dialogue, we are seeking to *create shared meaning* by connecting at the level of beliefs, values and feelings, or what is invisible. Dialogue enables us to get in touch with what informs our own and others' opinions and behaviour. It allows us to discover what is going on behind the scenes, shining light on a deeper truth. Through questioning, sharing feelings and giving each other full attention we find out who we are individually and collectively, without the make-up and the costumes. From here we have more power to create and provide the leadership for inspired performance.

The following are some suggested guidelines to promote a process of dialogue:

- Before talking – pause and reflect
- Adopt a 'learner's mind'
- Live with the silences
- Enquire with a *genuine desire* to know
- Speak only when *moved* to speak
- Withhold all judgements
- Use 'I' statements
- Be willing to be changed by what you hear
- Look for meaning, not for answers

'Adopting a spirit of enquiry is also an essential step in making successful behaviour change,' says Linda Logan Condon, an executive coach and a facilitator of open space dialogue. Only by examining our underlying assumptions, beliefs and values are we able to make the adjustments necessary to allow us to behave in different ways. If we fail to make this deeper examination any changes in behaviour will be short-lived.

A 'New' World

In this age, when we communicate through computers and video technologies with people thousands of miles away, there are growing desires for deeper connection. The sophistication of communication has been both a curse and a blessing. Some of the overuse and abuse of these processes is leaving little time for authentic communication. People talk about receiving a hundred or more e-mails a day. The system is used to copy everyone and their brothers in order to ensure that no one slips through the net. People sending these e-mails don't think about the relevance to the reader, but simply want to cover their own backsides! In some cases, people don't want to go on vacation because of the build-up of electronic messages. One client returned from ten days away to find 1,720 messages.

One of the most costly consequences of all of this electronic communication is that people find themselves with less time to spend with their customers and their employees in genuine conversations. Relationships suffer, and in the end so does productivity. The leadership of many companies would do well to invest time and energy in auditing these processes and developing guidelines to which people can be held accountable.

The purpose of communication is to build connections, to understand one another and to share perspectives. It takes time, and an investment of energy. It also takes wisdom to know that it is the myths and the storytelling that create cultural cohesion and align people with the organisation's mission.

As systems and processes are adapted to operate effectively in the *Relationship Age* it takes authentic leadership to introduce 'new stories' that are supportive of the changing nature of work. It takes a leadership orientation that focuses on the invisible energies to promote high-performance cultures and a spirit of cooperation. Any leaders who do not see this as their job are at risk of losing their legitimacy.

'Our people are our greatest asset' used to be one of the great management clichés, enshrined on the front of annual reports all over the corporate world. It seems that after all these years, the reality is finally catching up with the rhetoric. Results are still paramount, but leadership today has more to do with encouraging people to perform at the very best of their potential than with micro-managing every last detail.

Those leaders who are in touch with their inner authority build quality relationships, are honest and open in their communications and expect the same of others. They recognise that in these times of rapid transition to a global society, by continually expressing the truth they are freed to focus their energies on being of service to the broader enterprise.

The following are the Leadership capabilities needed to fully access the energy of the Fifth Key.

Leadership Capabilities

- Speaks and listens with deep respect
- Shares personal stories
- Operates with integrity
- Balances advocacy and enquiry – skilled in dialogue
- Stays fully present
- Aware of subtle nuances in communication like body language and facial expressions
- Tells the truth
- Talks about feelings

Global Implications

In a world where connection and communication are paramount to peace, we still have a great deal of room for improvement. Issues of integrity, and the lack of it, confront us daily on personal, organisational and global levels. With wars of ideology continuing to erupt around the world, it is clear that there are still too many cases in which the ego dominates, and where there is still unwillingness to truly listen to the wisdom in another's point of view.

The Need for Humility

There are indicators that the ground is becoming more fertile, and the deeper truth will emerge through genuine dialogue. However, this requires that leaders learn to relinquish the need to be 'right' and learn a little humility. In too many situations, the sense of righteousness prevails and the mentality of 'my opinion, my strategy, my God is better than yours' continues, with a reluctance to let go of traditional perspectives of power and control.

Electronic communication, global TV and a change in the

philosophy of some of the world's leaders are all placing greater emphasis on creating peace. As everyday people learn to connect with one another through the Internet and other forms of modern technology, the web of interdependence is strengthened and the truth of how life is in other parts of the world is revealed.

As we listen to the voices of hope and despair from those who have suffered, we cannot help but be touched by them, as can be seen from the numbers of people who are supporting others in their efforts to live lives of respect. With communication tools becoming so much more sophisticated and accessible to the masses, people are forming global focus groups of concerned citizens. They work together both electronically and by other means to eliminate the inequities and address issues of human dignity – www.thehungersite.com is just one example of how people are contributing.

As people become more conscious of their true identity through deeper enquiry, and have access to increasing levels of information, they are becoming more aware of the nature of the relationships needed to sustain the future. As the intolerance for global inequity and environmental degradation grows, there are increased pressures on public officials to live with integrity. The tolerance for conspiracy and corruption is lower than ever, and those who have considered themselves above the law are being called to task and their crimes brought into the light.

Now is a great time to create a new mythology for ourselves as a Global Society. It is time to tell a 'new story' that reflects the changing consciousness and provides the platform for a new way of living as a global community. Storytelling has always been a rich part of how history has been communicated from generation to generation. It is the foundation of every culture (ethnic, national and organisational) and has the power to either reinforce or change the status quo. The repeated myths and stories form the basis for the shared values and behaviours that create belonging. They are also much more than this. Michael Ray and Lorna Catford tell us that: 'Myths and stories are the reflection of the human soul. They remind us of our potential, of the divine possibilities of our existence.'

So what assumptions, values and behaviours do we need to begin sharing in order to build greater integration across the planet, align economics, ecology and religious ideologies and bring an end to war and suffering? How can we reflect the collective essence of humanity in ways that transform the way we live together here on Earth?

Clearly we are not there yet, and the 'scarcity assumption' still remains the master myth underlying the prevailing leadership paradigm, but people are changing. As we become more conscious of our interconnectedness and the need for higher levels of integrity, one of the values underpinning any new orientation to leadership has to be the communication of stories reflective of the deeper truth of the human spirit.

11

TRUSTING INTUITION

The only real valuable thing is intuition.
Albert Einstein

THE SIXTH KEY

Characteristics
Unlocked
Intuitive, imaginative, wise, visionary, seer, insightful, alert, flowing, perceptive, confused, non-linear, open-minded
Locked
Narrow-minded, tunnel vision, mentally imprisoned, obsessive thinking, recurrent nightmares, rigidity, untrusting, lost in logic

Personal Implications

THE SIXTH KEY FOR accessing the power of our authentic presence is often referred to as the third eye. It allows us to 'see' in ways that are very different from the view through our normal lenses. It is the doorway into the unconscious mind, where 'knowing' happens outside of our everyday awareness. Intuition is one of our greatest personal assets, and learning to trust it is a significant challenge in a society that places such high value on logic and linearity.

For centuries, intuition has been seen as a feminine characteristic, and it was once solely attributed to women. In the last thirty years it has become more widely appreciated, and is now recognised as an essential leadership ability that both sexes possess. This energy centre is also associated with inner knowing, remote viewing, telepathy, psychic powers, clairvoyance, precognition and automatic writing.

The Fifth Key opens the doorway that allows us to listen inwardly, and the Sixth Key unlocks our potential for inner seeing. When we open our 'inner eye' we awaken to the realisation that we are first and foremost spiritual beings, and that our deeper wisdom flows from a universal source that transcends logic. This energy centre takes us into the realms of intuitive insight that there are many ways to describe. In one way, intuition is a form of inner teaching and the illumination of a deeper truth. In another it's simply a way of accessing data without using the rational thought processes – we know without 'knowing'!

When we start *knowing* in these ways, we may feel a little alarmed as we receive information outside the normal channels. There are people who can see the past and the future, others who can read auras (the colourful energy field surrounding the body) and there are those who have a *sixth sense* about things. Some people are able to find their way to places without being given any direction, while others just get a strong pull to be at a certain place at a certain time.

Validating Imagination

Many of us as children had easy access to our intuition and the wisdom and insight of our inner teaching. Unfortunately, we were not always encouraged to trust in our deeper knowing because it wasn't logical. We were even taught to doubt our own experiences and intuitions because it didn't make rational sense and was thought of instead as a lot of 'non-sense'!

> Some years ago a colleague came to work one day feeling very bad about himself. He described how his four-year-old daughter had been talking to an old woman who appeared in her bedroom from time to time. As they sat over breakfast, the little girl had explained how the woman had visited her that morning to see how she was, and had talked with her before she got out of bed.
>
> My colleague chose to tell his daughter that it was merely her imagination playing tricks on her, and that she

> needed to stop thinking in these ways. The little girl was deeply saddened. He knew in his heart that what she was describing was real for her, and that it was only his fear that caused him to negate her experience. Because he didn't understand exactly what was happening in rational terms, he found it hard to accept.
>
> As he told us the story he suddenly realised that as her father he had the awesome power to cause her to doubt her own experience and discourage her from expressing her true self. Fortunately for this little girl, her father was open-minded enough to accept his own limiting beliefs. He returned home that evening determined to listen and hear more about his daughter's elderly companion.

There are many reasons why intuition and our ability to 'see' in non-ordinary ways are feared by some, and underdeveloped in many. The witch burnings that took place in Europe between the fifteenth and seventeenth centuries clearly impacted the acceptability of extra-sensory perception. Many of those burned were seers and healers working with the wisdom of the ages, and able to carry out apparent miracles.

One of the consequences of these times was that parents learned to protect their children by discounting their gifts of seeing and inner knowing, telling them that such things were the 'work of the devil'. These old myths and legends are still influencing us. Even now, in the twenty-first century, many people are still afraid of 'getting burned' by more traditional thinkers if they express this part of themselves.

Today, however, there is a significant trend towards wider acceptance of intuition and the less visible realm of spirit. In fact, looking at the increase in literature on metaphysics, as well as the demand for alternative approaches to life management, it's changing quite rapidly. The openness to what was once thought of as 'heretical' ideas is growing as we gain greater insight into human nature and the potential of our minds.

A Higher Intelligence

When we look back on our lives, all of us have stories that we can tell about the times we knew something was going to happen – and it did; or someone was going to telephone – and they did! Yet we think of these as random events, coincidences or a moment of chance. Having described them in these ways we discount our natural intuitive abilities, and fail to tap into the incredible wealth of data to which we have ready access.

The unconscious is constantly trying to get our attention. It sends us images, symbols and signals to wake us up to the potential we all have to become wise and to articulate ways that are different from our traditional schooling. However, our fears can cause us to think of all this as fantasy, or fiction, and to shut it away. If we are ever to claim the full potency of our leadership then we have to learn to trust and develop our intuitive capabilities.

In order to access the energy of this Key, and open to our deeper wisdom, we have to face the *fear of true knowing*. To do so means confronting our ambivalence about what this might tell us about who we think we are and the life we are living. The futurist Willis Harman wrote: 'We want to know where we are deceiving ourselves, but at the same time we will go to great lengths to avoid finding out. We have been thoroughly taught in Western culture not to trust ourselves – not to trust that ultimately we do know what we most deeply desire, and how to resolve our inner conflicts. We have been taught that beneath the thin veneer of the socialised conscious mind lurk who-knows-what animal urges, repressed hostilities and other evils. We have been taught not to risk exploring the unconscious mind – at least not without a psychiatrist seated alongside in case we should get into trouble.'

Once we overcome this fear and accept our authentic power, in a non-egocentric way, then we realise that every thought and every deed has consequence on the whole of creation. We take ownership of our full potential, discovering that there is nobody 'out there' to blame. We know, without a shadow of a doubt, that we are all connected to one another through a higher intelligence. We learn to dip into what Carl Gustav Jung referred to as the

Universal Unconscious, finding the wisdom that unites us irrespective of race, religion, social status or gender. With this sense of oneness as the ground of being, the need to operate with the mindset of alliance becomes obvious. The fundamental assumption of 'if somebody loses, nobody wins' makes perfect sense from this perspective.

Inner 'Knowing'

Roger Sperry, who won a Nobel Prize in 1981 for his pioneering work on the split-brain theory, ignited a great deal of new thinking in the area of intuition and non-linear processes. He observed that there were significant differences between the two hemispheres of the brain. Others have gone further by attributing certain characteristics to the right hemisphere and others to the left hemisphere. The right-brain is thought to work with symbolic language, emotion, music, patterns, intuition and holistic and divergent thinking. The left-brain focuses on logic, words, rational thought, deductive reasoning, cause and effect relationships and convergent thought processes.

The intuitive 'hit' or insight connects through the right-brain and the intellect of the left-brain transforms it into something concrete. More than this, there is a magic ingredient that results from this extraordinary synergy when it is connected with our soul's intention. It's as if this alignment brings a moment of enlightenment that allows us to reconcile all sense of duality, and to enter a state of simple knowingness. In these moments we have the experience of pure insight and connect to our true leadership power as co-creators of this reality.

Learning to trust our Self and the wisdom that comes from a place beyond logical understanding is a huge challenge. Once we have an understanding of the interrelatedness of all things, we touch a deeper knowing and rise above the dualistic impulses that lead us into the fear and isolation.

Breaking through these old patterns and opening our inner eyes can be immensely confronting, creating periods of intense emotional pain and confusion. Sometimes, when we are under significant emotional, mental and physical stress, we cross over the boundaries of sanity into a world that doesn't make a lot of sense to our rational minds. At some point, virtually everyone who embarks on a journey of soul-discovery experiences moments of madness. It's almost like a rite of passage to owning our full power. It's as if the balance of our mind has to be disturbed in order to shake us from our complacency and open us to new ways of seeing. At these times it's important to have a strong support system of people who can provide help when we lose clarity and get lost in the *dark*.

Today, rather than being seen as negative states of mind, many of these crises are seen as signs of growth, and an opening to expanded levels of awareness and higher intelligence. As a result there are many more places we can go to for help. Whether we are suffering from nightmares or depression, consumed by fear and terror or just out of our minds because we have lost all sense of purpose and direction, there are therapists, counsellors and social workers who can guide us to the other side. The importance of quality relationships, as well as expert help at such times, cannot be underestimated and can serve as a lifeline on the days when the sun forgets to shine.

Meditation is also an excellent means for both harmonising and rising above the pulls of Western living and for bringing the stillness needed to reconnect with our inner lights. Eastern mystics and yogis have known for centuries of its value and the peace that comes from quieting the busy mind. With so much emphasis and reward in the West on 'doing' coupled with the fear of what might happen if we were to stop and listen, we find a multitude of reasons for not taking the time to 'look within'. Instead, many of us are content to fill our lives with a steady stream of distractions, rather than to do the inner work necessary to claim our authentic leadership power

Waking Up

If we are one of the lucky ones, something or someone will gently nudge us into opening the door to the wisdom of our soul's knowing. If we are not, then it may well take a sledgehammer before we wake up! All too often, we wait until we are ill or emotionally out of sorts before we open our eyes to this deeper truth – sometimes this is what it takes. Yet when looking back how many of us can remember the little signals that we disregarded, the sudden thought or feeling that we dismissed or the twinge that we ignored.

Chloe had been working very hard to establish herself as a solid performer with significant potential. She was ambitious and enjoyed the sense of achievement she got from her work. She was very secure in her marriage, a relationship that she valued tremendously and that gave her the anchor she needed to feel balanced. One day without any prior warning her husband had a heart attack and died. Chloe was devastated. Although she knew it would be wise to slow down at work, instead she speeded up!

She increased the amount of travelling she was doing and got involved in a number of demanding projects. At first she was going to bed exhausted and sleeping very heavily, but after a while she couldn't sleep, and when she did, she began having vivid dreams. One was of a volcano erupting, and a second of a house being demolished. She was afraid, and would wake up panicking in the middle of the night feeling lost and lonely. She said she heard what she described as someone knocking on the door. She knew all of this was symbolic in some way but chose to ignore it by continuing to keep busy.

A year after the death of her husband she began getting severe migraines, which stopped her in her tracks. She couldn't function when they took over, and their frequency was increasing. It was at this point that she decided to take a four-week break, finally acknowledging what her intuition had been telling her for many months. Chloe described how she suddenly realised that she had to overcome her fear of finding out what she already knew, but didn't want to face up to. 'What I was doing to myself became more frightening than what I was trying to escape from.' In time, with professional support and her own commitment to becoming whole again, the migraines became less frequent and she found a new sense of security within herself.

The body is a great source of wisdom and is sending us messages, all the time, as to how we need to be happy and healthy. Too often we are unwilling to listen, because we're so caught up in all the 'doing' that our fear of 'knowing' gets in the way. So we wait for the headaches, the recurring infections, the accidents or the chronic diseases before we get serious about taking back our lives from all the diversions. At some point, the wake-up call *will* come for most of us; it's just a question of how many times we push the snooze button before we realise that the alarm has gone off for a reason!

We can also use the body to tune into what's going on around us by staying alert to its signals. Sometimes people get physical feelings that are trying to tell them about someone or something. If only we took the time to question what! Intuition is like a muscle that needs exercise, and with a little discipline becomes a really powerful asset. We're picking up data every second through our energy field, but our intellects are so busy solving problems in the same old way that we can fail to notice these subtler cues. On the occasions when we do stop and take note, many of us end up talking ourselves out of what our intuitions are telling us, rationalising to ourselves that we'd better stick with the facts.

Dreams are another source of information, allowing us to shine a light on the workings of the unconscious mind. There are different kinds of dreams – some are just a clearing of clutter from the day; others are much more than this. Dreams provide us with important insight into issues and opportunities that lie along our path, and are full of imagery and symbolism. Different animals have different meanings, as do numbers, and colours. Whether we dream of people, mountains, forests, houses, storms, cars or anything else, they all have some significance.

If you have vivid dreams then using your intuition to decipher their meaning is an important first step. Referring to books on dream interpretation can be of help, so too can consulting with someone who is skilled in this area. It's important to remember that only you as the dreamer know the true meaning of the dream.

The Value of Vision

The Sixth Key is connected with the spiritual *value of vision* – a word that, until recently, was related only to our physical eyes, or used in religious teachings, such as having a celestial vision, or an experience of God. With the wider availability of hallucinogens in the 1960s, people found themselves 'seeing' in different ways. Psychologists and psychiatrists carried out extensive research to understand the effect of these drugs on our brains and our psyches. New disciplines emerged as the spiritual dimension and transpersonal realms became more vivid and accessible, and personal growth became more highly valued.

Another way of thinking of vision is as the gift of insight that allows us to deepen our wisdom and to access even more of the power of our soul's expression. This Key opens the doorway to active spiritual engagement. It is here that we develop the *relationship with our inner guidance* and connect with what some refer to as their guides and guardians, which accompany us on our life's journey. Visualisation exercises are of real value to begin the process of receiving guidance from other sources. Such support and encouragement is invaluable, when we are faced with our fears along the path of enlightenment.

People who work actively with the energy of this centre are open to less conventional ways of learning. The language of vision encourages the use of symbolism, such as the Tarot, astrology, numerology, the runes and other 'universal toys' that may provide insight. Over the past ten years, increasing numbers of people in business are exploring the world of symbols, mythology and metaphor to help them professionally and personally. More and more are consulting psychics, spiritual healers and astrologers to provide them with alternative 'perspectives' on reality. Each of us, however, has to take care that we don't become too dependent on these outside points of view and so forget to trust and develop our own intuition as the source of our most powerful and fulfilling visions.

A World of Colour

Another strong influence on the brightness of our energy and the power of our presence is the whole area of light and colour. This has a significant effect on the pineal gland and helps to regulate the body's circadian rhythm. People who suffer from Seasonal Affective Disorder (SAD) often experience being high in the summer and low in the winter. These conditions are triggered by changes in the amount of light and darkness, which in turn affect the levels of serotonin and melatonin in the body. People who are intuitive are often more sensitive to these changes and need to trust in a process of release and renewal: holding on to outdated patterns which do not support a lightness of being will in time drive the sparkle from their spirits and their ability to be effective. Meditation can help greatly in maintaining the body's well-being at these times.

There are some more common phrases that we link to colour. We talk of being green with envy, or seeing red when we're angry. When we're down we talk about feeling blue, and someone who is cowardly is called yellow. There are colours associated with each of the energy centres. Richard Gerber says in his book *Vibrational Medicine*: 'The opening and proper functioning of the third eye is usually seen in those who are highly developed at the intuitive level. The colour indigo resonates most forcefully with this centre. Indigo appears to control physical and higher aspects of vision as well as olfaction (smell) and hearing.'

Other colours have influence on us, and although there are different points of view, the following provides an example:

- red – security, warmth
- orange – activity, vitality
- yellow – power, nourishment
- green – renewal, healing
- blue – calming, cooling
- indigo – inspiring, creative
- purple – higher consciousness, revelation

As we face the limitations of the prevailing paradigm in describing our personal experiences of reality, the desire for deeper understanding of the spiritual and psychic realms grows. The importance of accessing our intuitive abilities and understanding symbolic language is key to claiming our full leadership potential.

All of us are intuitive and more of us are learning how to apply this skill in our daily lives. The more we trust it, and tune in to the spiritual direction that helps us to stay connected to our soul's purpose, the healthier and more rounded we will become. Working to develop our power of vision, and our skills in guided visualisation can be enormously effective in accessing the increased levels of energy needed to contribute leadership in today's world.

Key Questions

- What happens when you listen to your intuition? What happens if you don't?
- How does your intuition help you with your learning?
- What brings your imagination to life?
- How open are you to the signals your body sends you?
- When are you clearest about your personal vision?
- Are you living your dream?
- How does your fear of 'true knowing' get in your way?

Organisational Implications

As we walk the hallways of some of our most prestigious organisations and are confronted by the colourless walls, rectangular offices and windowless meeting rooms, we must be careful not to allow ourselves to be deceived. For underneath the grey facade lies a wealth of colourful imagination that is beginning to bubble to the surface. I am happy to report that intuition is alive and well in organisations, but often operating undercover!

The Myers Briggs Type Indicator has helped to legitimise intuition as an important component of managerial life. In the early

1990s, a colleague and Fellow of the World Business Academy, Jagdish Parikh, carried out research into the use of intuition in decision-making. His findings were surprising and supportive of the statement above. Over seventy-five per cent of the managers interviewed 'confessed' that in the majority of cases, their decisions were made intuitively and then supported with a rational analysis. Peter Senge also found from his work that: 'Very often experienced managers have rich intuitions about complex systems, which they cannot explain. Their intuitions tell them that cause and effect are not close in time and space, that obvious solutions will produce more harm than good and that short-term fixes produce long-term problems. But they cannot explain their ideas in simple linear cause–effect language.'

My own experiences confirm these findings, and it seems that it is a good time for leadership to put intuition on a par with reason in institutional settings. By recognising and rewarding intuition we can open the doorway to the skills and abilities that will nurture a new orientation to leadership in a world of increasing complexity. Time wasted in rationalising decisions to make them more palatable is costing companies a lot of money, especially when speed and decisiveness are of the essence. In fact, legitimising the role of intuition will inevitably help to promote greater accountability for decision-making and increased commitment. People can then focus on achieving results and not on trying to justify each step they take.

Allowing Chaos

Organisations need 'breakthrough thinking' in order to ensure a process of ongoing renewal. A number of leaders are still resisting the natural flow of energy by attempting to control it. They are unwilling to let go of justifying, analysing and quantifying everything. They are scared of the chaos that they think would emerge if they allowed people to connect to their intuition and work together in new ways.

> The company had just celebrated its fiftieth anniversary. The CEO had grown up in the organisation and was dedicated

to its continued growth. He was highly thought of and people had a great deal of respect for his perspective. As a result of some major market changes the performance of the company began to falter. The senior management knew that they needed to engage in a significant change process if they were going to meet the shareholders' expectations. The CEO, however, thought this wasn't necessary. He made it clear that he supported incremental change and that it was all that was needed to ensure success.

Others knew differently. Their intuition was sending them clear signals that the only way to secure the longer-term health of the organisation was to engage in a process of transformational change. However, the resistance to change expressed by their boss held them back and became increasingly costly to the company. Good people started to leave while others became disillusioned. Cost-cutting became a way of life with no clear vision guiding the strategic choices that were being made. The absence of an overarching vision that allowed people to see the future direction became all too obvious as the various functions and businesses struggled to determine how best to operate in such an environment.

The CEO seemed to be guided by the numbers and was unable to 'see' a picture of a future that was significantly different from the past. Without this he couldn't in all conscience support the transformation of the enterprise because he saw no purpose. Even with the help of his top team he could not be convinced of the need for change.

The chaos that is generated as a result of ongoing cycles of death and rebirth, release and renewal are essential parts of organisational life. Like any organism that ceases to be open to these natural dynamics of growth, it will decay. The fear of chaos and the unwillingness to trust the process of transformation shuts out the light in both individuals and organisations.

Creating a Container

One of the most critical leadership capabilities in this time of alliances, mergers and acquisitions is the ability to create an environment for change that is safe enough to allow the old to break down and the new to emerge. This requires building a 'container' in which the process of change can occur.

The best metaphor for describing the function of the 'container' is that of the transformation of the caterpillar into the butterfly. The chrysalis or cocoon forms a 'container' that protects the caterpillar as it disintegrates. It provides the safe space for the old structure to break down and the new one to form. Transformation is a process that takes time, patience and trust, and if the container or the chrysalis is opened prematurely the butterfly or new organisational form will perish.

The parallel between this metaphor and the change process in organisations is obvious. All too often, time is not given for the 'new order' to emerge, especially when the focus is predominantly on short-term results. Managers who are driven by shareholders to achieve quarterly targets cannot possibly be champions of change and provide the container needed to allow transformation to happen. The consequences are clear, we read about them every day in the business sections of the newspapers. Either the organisation remains stuck in 'caterpillar consciousness', or the 'container' is cracked prematurely by impatience and short-termism, and the potential of what might have been is lost. In the end, everyone including the investors pays a high price for the pressure they put on companies to make fast money.

Inspiration and Vision

For the past thirty years there has been increasing amounts of data to suggest that leadership has a lot more to do with inspiration, vision and the championing of change than with straightforward technical competence. The ambitious, over-qualified high-flier with a flawless track record who gets stuck in managing minutiae will soon be left behind.

Today, more than ever, a premium is being placed on a magic

ingredient that is hard to define. Leadership has to do with 'presence' and with subtle energies – something substantive yet unquantifiable. We know when it's there in someone and we know when it's not! We find it in the person whose energy is both dynamic and magnetic, who is able to integrate reason and intuition and who respects themselves and others.

These people are those that inspire us, and who are able to shine a light on the road ahead. They are in touch with the authentic power that comes from their soul's authority. They are able to communicate their commitment to a vision to others, providing the feeling that we are all in this together. Such people promote a sense of oneness of purpose, and generate energy to the possibilities of what could be. They are not limited by what is. These are the true visionaries who are able to capture the hearts and minds of people in ways that are free from fear and dictatorial edicts. They 'turn us on' and are the bright lights that encourage each of us to live true to our vision of what is possible.

In the 1960s, 'vision' began to gain popularity as a way of inspiring large numbers of people to look beyond the current reality into a world of possibility. The Americans John F. Kennedy and Martin Luther King were thought of as visionary leaders of a new era. They were able to capture people's imaginations and promote a vision of shared accountability that was quite different from the past. Later, in the 1970s and 1980s, 'vision' became common business parlance, as thousands of people engaged in visioning retreats. They created vision statements, departmental visions, team visions and organisational visions!

As a result the notion of 'modern-day visionaries' emerged in the working world, and visioning became a critical leadership competency. It is a process that is both used and abused today. What it has served to do is to open the door into 'higher intelligence' and the possibilities for transforming the working environment.

Over the years many organisational visions come and many go. Listed below are several factors that seem to give a vision more potency.

- The vision has to ignite a fire strong enough to transform deep-seated beliefs and assumptions that are restricting growth.
- The vision has to be created using intuition and a system-thinking lens, not just through cause-and-effect thinking.
- Every person must feel connected to the vision, holding it in their mind's eye as they go about their daily work.
- The vision has to be grounded in concrete action and not simply held as an idealised state – it has to be realisable moment by moment.
- People have to feel that what they are doing *matters* in the grand scheme of things if a vision is to inspire hearts and minds and achieve organisational excellence.
- The vision has to draw on the collective wisdom of the entire organisation or 'organism'.

Visioning, done properly, and supported by higher values and authentic behaviour, has enormous power to channel the energy of the organization in a common direction. Such a process promotes alignment and cohesion, and connects individual members and the disparate parts of an organisation to one another, in ways that are enlivening.

Legitimising Intuition

The potential of the Sixth Key to unlock untold levels of authentic leadership power is boundless. The intuitive and psychic energies that people possess are just waiting to be legitimised in organisational settings, if only we had the inspired leadership to establish the appropriate context. I have had many conversations with top managers, who have access to these abilities, yet who are afraid to talk about their intuitions through fear of ridicule when they get together with their colleagues. The collusion to keep this 'deeper knowing' in the dark is significant; but the need to allow its expression has never been so necessary. The energy of this Key is a critical factor in determining those companies that will succeed and those that will fail in the coming years.

Without the use of intuition, organisations will be unable to move quickly enough to renew themselves and to face the multiplicity of challenges that are emerging in the multicultural society. Logic, linearity and cause-and-effect relationships only represent one side of the equation. Any institution that relies too heavily on this orientation is likely to find itself operating in isolation. If there is a predominance of this thinking, then the focus will be on maintaining structure and separation and not on promoting connection and alignment. Those that are opening themselves to using intuition more overtly, and who see the value of ritual and symbolism in freeing the power of the human spirit, are learning to ride the waves of change.

The potential and the need for enlightened leadership have never been greater. In talking with individuals, I feel excited at the possibilities for whole new ways of working together. However, for this transformation to really happen we have to find the courage to trust our inner teaching and what we know to be so. We have to learn to integrate wisdom and intellect in ways that honour the natural cycle of decay and regeneration.

The following are the leadership capabilities to activate the energy of this key:

Leadership Capabilities

- Unafraid to dream
- Patient with the natural rhythms of life
- In touch with inner vision
- Creates out of the chaos
- Takes time for meditation
- Inspires the imagination of people
- Encourages the use of intuition
- Supports others in realising their personal dreams

Global Implications

One Man's Vision

In September 1995, Jim Garrison began to realise his vision of creating a forum to bring together 'the creative genius of the human family, its elders and innovators in a search for solutions to the critical challenges facing humanity in the twenty-first century'. The first of those gatherings was held in San Francisco that same year, and brought together political, scientific, spiritual and business leaders from all over the world – Nobel Prize winners, heads of state, spiritual masters, eminent scientists, business executives, Hollywood stars and representatives of the world's youth population. This extraordinary collection of people assembled with the sole purpose of developing a global agenda.

This was the first time that this collection of individuals had ever been in the same room together, and the energy that was generated was amazing. People like Mikhail and Raisa Gorbachev, Buddhist monk Thich Nhat Hahn, scientist Carl Sagan, primatologist Jane Goodall, business magnate Ted Turner, actresses Shirley MacLaine and Jane Fonda, South African President Thabo Mbeke and Nobel Laureate Oscar Aria Sanchez were all there to participate in a dialogue to catalyse the emergence of a new Global Ethic.

Now, after nine years, the State of the World Forum is a thriving network of people connected by a 'unique matrix of shared values and ideas'. Something that began as one man's vision has generated the commitment of many thousands of people from diverse cultures and disciplines who are actively engaged in 'co-creating a better world for humanity and all living things'. In 2000, the 'gathering' was held in New York in connection with the United Nations Millennium Summit – the largest meeting of heads of state in modern history.

The Vision of a State of the World Forum was a big one and one with a clear champion who has enormous commitment to a higher purpose. I believe the greatest compliment I can pay to Jim Garrison is to tell you that he is not really any different from you and me. He simply trusted in his inner knowing and claimed his authentic leadership power to make a contribution.

We are all intuitive and gifted visionaries if we believe we are. We can all dream of what a world of peace and plenty would look like. And in many ways, that's exactly what we each need to do. The elements and form of our vision and the nature of our contribution will be different from Jim's, but the intent can be the same.

The Missing Piece

Many of the dilemmas we are facing today are a result of the absence of communication of a cohesive global vision. We don't have a shared picture of our collective future, and rather like being without the picture on the lid of the jigsaw-puzzle box, we find it hard to imagine how everything fits together. We each need to turn inwards to see how our unique piece fits in the context of the whole. The State of the World Forum and other similar communities are helping people engage in such a process and helping us to envision our role in creating a global society.

Intuitively we all know that the future depends on our abilities to create greater alignment and cohesion. Not sameness or uniformity, but a world where economic, ecological and social issues have equal weight, and where people matter as much as wealth and power. We have some way to go but we have at least begun. The challenge is made even greater because of the bombardment of visual images and verbal messages from the media, telling everyone how the more they have, the happier they will be! The brain is constantly absorbing this data and we have to have a great deal of awareness to remain alert to the truth of our inner reality, when the outside influences are so strong.

It's sad to see how Western ways are beginning to eradicate the cultural identities of other nations. If we allow this to continue without consciousness, we will lose the richness of diversity. In addition, if people all over the world are led to believe that the accumulation of wealth is the only true path to happiness, we will witness an acceleration in the rate of depletion of the Earth's natural resources and a greater threat to our collective survival.

When Sperry's theories of the left and right hemispheres of the brain first came to my awareness, I realised the globe could be viewed loosely in a similar way. The Western or left hemisphere has a bias towards linearity and logic, technical competence, a preference for activity and a focus on the physical world, whereas the Eastern or right hemisphere has always been known for its richness of spirit, deep wisdom, and use of colour, costume and ritual.

If we seek to strengthen the connections between these two hemispheres, we can have the best of all worlds and open the space in which our collective power can emerge. Together, we can find ways to share the differing nature of our 'wealth' with each other. We know that the West is hungry for a spiritual reawakening and parts of the East could gain from increased technical competence. The potential is obvious and the willingness is growing stronger.

A Sharing of Wisdom

There are people today who are actively seeking ways to bring the Eastern and Western traditions together in ways that benefit both, and to create enriched perspectives and disciplines. One example of where it is happening to the benefit of all is in the healing traditions. Chinese acupuncture, Indian Ayurvedic medicine, yoga, qi gong and reiki are just some examples. They deal a lot more with subtle energies, including the relationship of emotional and spiritual energy to our well-being, while conventional Western medicine focuses primarily on the physical and mental body alone. Complementary medicine is gaining in popularity in the West as people face the limitation of allopathic approaches that involve drugs and surgery. In the same way, certain of our Western methods are bringing help and hope to people in other parts of the world.

There are some, however, who are opposed to the ancient traditions on the grounds of quackery and credibility. Despite this resistance, significant changes are taking place, especially in the whole area of visualisation and the mind–body connection. A desire for a greater understanding of the world of metaphysics and spiritual understanding has been growing in popularity over the past thirty years. Books about spiritual insight, intuition, magic and mysticism are frequently found on the top of best-seller lists.

With a heavy orientation to the mechanistic mindset, the West has been slow in acknowledging the rituals and symbolism, which we know, intuitively, allow us to maintain a healthy relationship to the world around us. Many of the ceremonies, like the solstice celebrations, that encouraged people to enter alternative realities and to connect more deeply with their spiritual natures were eliminated as the scientific paradigm gained supremacy. Today, in the United Nations and the White House, in governments, corporations, schools and community gatherings, ritual and symbolism are returning. The American Indians, as well as other indigenous peoples, have brought many of their ancient traditions to the more structured minds of institutional settings. Vision quests, pipe ceremonies, sweat lodges and the medicine wheel are just some examples.

The Chinese art of feng shui is also growing in popularity in both personal and professional settings. People are becoming more curious and seeking to understand the wisdom behind other systems of thinking and living, recognising that they can add significant depth and meaning to their current reality. The global sharing has begun, and as people seek to integrate Spirit more fully into their lives, the awareness of intuition and its importance in maintaining vitality is growing.

HONOURING THE MYSTERY

I have the most exciting and compelling Invitation to walk in wonder and awe in to the mystery.
Guy Dosher

THE SEVENTH KEY

Characteristics
Unlocked
Conscious, enlightened, mystical, inspiring, humble, prophetic, devoted, liberated, silent
Locked
Purposeless, disconnected, lost, judgemental, restless, depressed, spiritually unaware, despairing, hopeless

Personal Implications

PERHAPS MY BIGGEST CHALLENGE in writing this book is to describe the qualities of the authentic leadership power accessed by this Key, because the Mystery, by its nature, is indescribable! However, as with the others the following is designed to give a flavour of the energies and the challenges that we can expect when we focus our attention here.

The Seventh Key opens the door to the world that lies beyond the known, where we are asked to relinquish all sense of attachment and jump naked into the abyss. Our awareness of a sense of unity becomes all-pervasive, as we consciously connect to the Source of life. There is no path to follow, because we have arrived. We live at the edge of our own discovery, creating out of the void. Our lights are on, we are fully conscious, living in the eternal now. We recognise that there is only the illusion of separation, and that in reality we are one with all that is. We experience a spiritual high as we let go and learn to live in the Mystery.

We have all touched moments like these and experienced the deep sense of peace when we give up control and let the Mystery take us. We just know when we are in the right place, at the right time, with the right people. We don't have to think about things, they just seem to happen, as if by magic. Such a moment can be triggered by a sunset, a wonderful meal, a chance meeting in an airport, the perfect golf swing or a sudden insight. For an instant we step outside ourselves and see something in a different light. It's happened to all of us.

Just imagine what life would be like if we allowed our lives to be this way more of the time rather than just an occasional happening. After all, *A Course in Miracles* tells us 'that miracles are natural, it's when they don't happen that you need to worry'. If we are to pass through this doorway and access the full potency of our leadership we have first to face the *fear of not knowing* and surrender to something that is beyond understanding. We need to learn to trust there is a benevolent force that is always operating in our highest good, if only we can stay out of our own way.

Taking the Leap

Letting go of the patterns and behaviours that perpetuate the way we are, especially when they don't serve our growth (to die to ourselves every night and be reborn each morning), this is the energy of the Seventh Key. To allow ourselves to look through new eyes time after time, trusting our soul to guide us, is a tough challenge in our ego-driven society. Instead of holding on to the known and trying to massage, manipulate, reshape or reconfigure it, we have to free ourselves from the bonds of obsessive thinking and repetitive patterns. Once we learn to 'let go and let God', abandoning ourselves to the Mystery, then we create the space that allows the true power of our presence to shine through.

This is probably the most scary and most liberating experience we can ever have as human beings, because such an experience demands the ultimate relinquishment of our attachment to fear. In these moments, we are invited to have faith in the unknown and to introduce the ingredient that completes the alchemical process – unconditional love. Nothing in the external world may change, but this shift in consciousness and the transformation of energy influence the whole cellular structure of our physical body. The vibration of the subtler energy fields takes on a wholly different quality of radiance to make us feel healthy and fully alive.

In practical terms, to evoke the fullness of our authentic leadership power means remaining ever-vigilant of the behavioural and thinking habits that keep us from allowing the power and beauty of the Mystery to enter our lives. To reach this point means practising the art of discernment, knowing when to hold on and when to let go. We have to relinquish the need to always be in control of everything that we think supports our concept of perfection, and which, more often than not, only serves to limit the potential of what is possible. It's a tough challenge, yet when we stop 'trying' to make life happen in a certain way, anything becomes possible. The universal flow takes over and wonderful synchronicities and coincidences occur as if by magic.

People who take this leap of faith often experience something that feels like the death of one state of consciousness and the birth of another. Some describe how they have 'seen the light', while others talk about touching heaven or reaching nirvana. Others tell of leaving their bodies and looking upon their physical being from the outside, or of a profound awakening, seeing in ways they've never seen before.

Such experiences change the perception of our lives forever. We cannot go back to the way we were before, because we now know that there is so much more to life that we don't 'know'! We have touched the unknowable and are forever changed. We have emerged from the chrysalis and our wings are outstretched. The energies of this Key take us from being self-conscious into the realms of universal consciousness. We find ourselves feeling that life, and all that goes with it, is a blessing. Even the tough stuff is there for a very good reason – to help us remember the truth of what we already know.

Creating A Personalised Concept of God

I remember when I was living in Calgary, Canada, in the early 1980s, I found myself struggling to understand a concept of God that worked for me. I had become disillusioned with what I once thought to be true, not even wanting to use the word because it didn't make sense anymore. One morning while taking a bath I got quite angry and confused as I thought about it all. A little while later I was staring out of the apartment window, far into the distance, when out of the blue I found myself 'seeing' in my mind's eye an enormous body of light – like the sun with billions of rays.

Each ray represented a person, a soul that had taken on human form to experience life on Earth. Those with their backs to the centre looking outwards along the ray identified more with separation and disconnection, because that's what they saw, while those focusing inwards, towards the core, saw unity and connection. What dawned on me in that moment was the realisation that each of us has been given free will to move along the ray as we wish. The further away from the source of light, the more distant we are from one another and the darker life becomes. The closer we are to the centre, the brighter the light and the more in touch we are with our co-creative power.

The more I thought about all of this, the more I began to wonder.

- *What if* the only real choice we have in life is how separate we want to feel from this great Source of Light?
- *What if* each soul develops a contract with the Universe to engage in certain experiences, and when we lose touch with this sense of destiny, we feel lonely and uninspired, lost in the dark?
- *What if* once we make the choice to reawaken to Spirit, we unlock the door to the experience of bliss, merging and separating at will with the Grace of God?

To find our own deeper mysteries takes consciousness and discipline, and to reach this place means embarking on a journey that takes us to the very core of our being, where we are asked to let go of all knowing. It means claiming back our lives from the myriad of conflicting beliefs and ideals with which our egos are programmed – and facing our shadow. We have to release any repressed emotions and learn how to live with awareness. Feelings are then acknowledged as they arise and are released in a healthy expression. We learn to recognise how this powerful source of energy can be transmuted into light, as a force that ignites our authentic leadership power.

Making Peace with Death

A factor that holds many of us back from experiencing the fullness of this spiritual journey is our Western concept of death. We have made death an enemy, and in so doing live life constantly under its shadow. We spend hundreds and thousands of dollars keeping people on life support, not wanting to let them go, sometimes against their will. If someone asks to die, we judge them as having diminished responsibility, or not in their right minds. We often override their wishes to die with dignity, because we find it so hard to accept that they would want to 'shed this mortal coil'.

Death of course is the ultimate Mystery, and if we adopt more of an Eastern orientation, physical life becomes a transitionary state that we may return to time after time on our paths to enlightenment. In fact, the whole notion of reincarnation was also a central teaching of the Christian faith until AD 325, when the Council of Nicaea chose to remove it from their teachings. It still, however, remains a core concept in many world religions.

The idea that the soul is eternal and returns many times to learn its lessons is a belief that is becoming more popular in Western culture. This is reflected in much of the current literature on spirituality, personal growth and transpersonal psychology. Past-life regression, hypnosis, spontaneous recall, soul retrieval and shamanic journeying are all experiences that are drawing more attention as people seek to understand the deeper meaning of life and confront their fear of dying.

Our resistance to change is also reflective of our relationship to death. People, who are afraid to initiate the needed changes in their lives, are more often than not, dealing with a deep-seated fear of facing their own mortality. Change by its nature gives us the experience of a 'mini-death', and unless we have a clear vision or deep faith in Spirit, it is hard to jump into the void. So instead many avoid change, unable to see it as part of the natural cycle of death and rebirth. This restricts the energy for living and allows fear to control our choices. Some of us hold on to jobs, to relationships and to situations long after they have come to a natural end. We are unaware that our own fear of death (or of *really* living) is causing us to remain stuck in something that no longer brings us joy and vitality.

Until we reframe the whole nature of death and dying, and see this as a core component of life, we are unlikely to live fully in the present moment. Once we are able to acknowledge our fear and yet remain free from attachment, we arrive at the place of total awareness. We know without a shadow of a doubt the truth of the statement that 'I do not live inside my body but the body is in me'. We connect with the great 'I am' or the big Self, and recognise that emotions, beliefs and behaviours are not all of who we are. They are merely facilitative of our soul's journey through life. We realise that change and letting go are essential to our ongoing spiritual realisation – and that it is a personal choice as to how we experience it – we can either serve or suffer.

The Value of Faith

> In 1998, two friends of mine, Bob and Michelle, decided to take a ride across America on their Harley Davidson motorcycles. It sounded like a wonderful adventure and they invited me to go with them. Bob was sixty and had been riding for two years. In November 1997 he had a near fatal accident, and after recovering he got right back on his bike. He had only ever carried a passenger a short distance. I knew all this and yet decided to ride on the back

with him. I was intoxicated by the sense of adventure and denied any fear. It was a 2,000-mile journey from Seattle, Washington to Traverse City, Michigan. We planned to ride for twelve days, staying at ranches and bed and breakfasts across the country.

I was so excited! I had all the gear and found myself relatively relaxed on the back of the bike, ignoring the undercurrent of fear that I knew had to be present on some level. On the fourth day, Bob dropped me outside a restaurant and went to park. As I stood there admiring the elegance of this powerful machine, the bike got caught in some loose gravel and Bob took a spill. Fortunately, it was a light fall and Bob was unhurt but our dinner conversation was very different from the night before. Michelle asked me how I felt, and I voiced my fear for the first time.

The next day as we set off, I was terrified! I sat on the back of the bike trying to guide and control Bob's every move – I was scared and not enjoying it one little bit. The thought of another eight days of seeing death round every corner was excruciating. After a few hours of riding, I was exhausted and fell into a daze. In that moment, I received a significant insight – *I had choice.* I knew that Bob could in no way avoid picking up my stress, I was only inches away from him and my whole energy field was full of fear. I thought about the effect that it must be having on him and recognised how easily it could all become a self-fulfilling prophecy. But how could I release the fear and relax again?

As soon as I asked the questions, the answer came back that I needed to stop investing energy in the fear, and to open up to faith in something greater than myself. Faith had never been a word I understood until that moment, when I let go of trying to control Bob, my fear, and my life and surrendered to a force far greater and far wiser than I.

Yes, the possibility of death was still very much there,

> as it is every moment we're alive. I learned that day that faith in the unseen, coupled with the belief that I am responsible for my experience of life, however long or short it might be, transcends fear. As this realisation sank in, I felt the flow of energy return to my tense little body, and shift my whole orientation to one that was more loving and respectful of Bob and myself. By the end of the trip, much to my surprise I was so relaxed I was able to drift off on the back of the bike!

The Seventh Key liberates us, opening the door to a very different awareness, in which we recognise we can consciously choose where to focus our energy in every moment. Neale Donald Walsch states clearly in *Conversations with God Volume 1*: 'Every single free choice you ever undertake arises out of only two possible thoughts there are: a thought of love or a thought of fear. Every human thought, word or deed, is based in one emotion or the other. You have no choice about this, because there is nothing else from which to choose. But you have free choice about which of these to select.'

Our work while we are here is to reawaken to this truth, to have faith in a benevolent universe, taking responsibility for the part we play in this extraordinary mosaic of life. To see our interrelationship with everything, knowing that when we judge someone else, we are really judging ourselves; when we hurt someone else, we are only hurting ourselves.

As we open our hearts to the light that shines through everyone, we allow the disparate parts of ourselves to come together. And, as each soul remembers the higher purpose of life, spirit and matter are reunited forming a web of interconnectedness that supports and sustains us. This is wholeness, to return to a place of peace and contentment. To come home and surrender to the Mystery.

Coming Home

People who operate predominantly from the Seventh Key are sometimes seen as gurus, mystics and holy men and women like Lao

Tsu, Jesus Christ, Sai Baba, Guru Mai, Buddha, Mother Meera, Mohammed and Krishna. Others are medicine men and women like the Kahunas in Hawaii, and the shamans of the indigenous populations. These people are wisdom teachers who can help us find the peace we need to be whole and create a personal alliance with God. They can assist us in retrieving those parts of our soul that are 'lost' or disowned, and guide us across the abyss that lies between who we think we are and who we truly are. If, however, we become overly attached or dependent on our 'guru', or upon any religious dogma, we are at risk of seeing another's perception of God, not our own.

This key opens the door to having an intimate union with the Source. We experience God as ultimate reality, with no fear or loss, simply the release of attachment to separation, as we blend our soul with the Source. Here we arrive at a place of no boundaries where all is pure consciousness. This is the experience of bliss. We know we have returned home, we surrender all our pain and we yield up all our suffering, held in the abundant unconditional love that is the Grace of God. The experience is nothing more and nothing less than everything. The search is over, the battle won, we remember what we forgot, and in that remembering, find inner peace and deep contentment.

Many of us have touched this for moments, releasing all ego identification and losing ourselves in the swirling serenity of this ecstatic embrace from the Universe. The challenge is to return here as often as we can, and to see this as the true source of our authentic power. Prayer and meditation are two of the finest ways of strengthening the *relationship to divine intelligence*. Talking with God through prayer and listening to God through meditation keep us in constant connection with our spiritual essence. Also, making love wholeheartedly can open the doorway to experiencing God in the most wonderful of ways as we abandon ourselves in a process of merging with another. Expressing the qualities of compassion, gratitude, kindness and forgiveness are other ways to deepen our experiences of our divinity.

Much in our society tells us we are unworthy of the happiness that comes from being one with all that is. There are many of us so filled with fear, guilt and shame that it is hard to allow this experience. Abraham Maslow, in his work on self-actualisation, describes this as the *Jonah complex*, or a fear of flying. As we get closer to actualising, we start to self-sabotage, afraid of the joy and the ecstasy, and feeling unworthy of the abundance of light and love that is the Source of life. Once we relinquish our attachments to suffering and simply surrender, allowing the flow of radiant energy to carry us where it will, we open ourselves to the Great Mystery. We touch the wellspring of Universal Love, merging with it and experiencing the oneness of everything. There is nothing to do anymore, the essence of this Key is pure being.

Key Questions

- What brings you peace?
- When are you most connected with life?
- What do you do to help others connect to more of a universal perspective?
- When did you make friends with death?
- What does reverence for life mean to you?
- Do you believe in miracles? When was your first experience of a miracle?
- How might 'fear of the unknown' get in your way?

Organisational Implications

With such a strong emphasis on structure and control, it's hard to imagine an awareness of the need for Honouring the Mystery in the world of institutions! There are, however, pockets of more enlightened leaders who are looking for new ways to free the innovative spirit in the workplace. These people are not satisfied with continuous improvement alone, they see opportunities for deep levels of transformation and the creation of brand-new products, business lines and markets.

The concept of Open Space developed by Harrison Owen is becoming more widely accepted in the business arena. This transformational technology provides a minimal framework that is paradoxically flexible and very concrete. With the help of a skilled facilitator people engage in meaningful dialogue on subjects they determine to be important to them. This often leads to greater awareness of both the opportunities and the blocks to an organisation's renewal. The door opens to the possibility for deeper levels of transformation to take place and to release the energy trapped in old patterns of leadership behaviour.

The challenge, which is especially great for those in senior management roles, is to let go of needing to 'know' what works best, and to open the space for something new to emerge. Only by creating such an opportunity is there a possibility to free the energy held back in the unconscious organisational patterns that are inhibiting growth. This three-stage process of breaking out, breaking down and breaking through is the ongoing cycle that enables the release of energy from tired structures. It creates the space for a new form to emerge more supportive of continuous growth and renewal.

Trusting in the Process

To trust in this process of transformation takes a great deal of faith and consciousness. The ability to live in the void, not knowing what the 'new' will truly be like, is a skill few of us possess. The irony is that we never *really* know what the outcome of anything will be. We live believing that we are in control, when from a place of pure logic it is so easy to see that there are far too many variables for anyone to truly know. We fill the place of 'not knowing' with busyness and copious plans for every contingency, pretending that everything is 'under control'!

Today, more than ever, people who hold tight to 'knowing and controlling' are likely to be the biggest blocks to effectiveness. As change speeds up, the consequences of these behaviours become even more perilous. Leaders who are fearful of change and are unwilling to let go and trust the process are severely limiting the growth of their enterprises.

To live in the Mystery in an organisational context sounds like asking an alligator to whistle, but without moments where this can happen, the creative genius of the organisation gets put into the shadows and before long the 'lights' will go out! The role of leadership in today's environment is to work with the energy dimensions of the organisation, ensuring that the structures transform quickly enough to serve the evolving purpose and direction.

The only way to do this is to ensure that the quality of relationships is so strong that they can be sustained without a firm structure. People need to be connected to one another by a sense of shared purpose or intention and not defined by form. Then they can continue to operate effectively as the structure continuously shifts its shape.

Organisational Wizardry

The Seventh Key energies naturally reinforce the characteristics of the alliance mindset, creating a platform that both promotes a unified focus, and values diversity as a prerequisite to creative synergy. People with this mindset have a sense of adventure and enjoy living on the edge, opening the space for differences to be expressed, in order to support higher levels of effectiveness. They have accessed their authentic leadership power and are skilled in the art of organisational wizardry. They are awake to the part of themselves that sees the magic of the human experience. These people know that:

- You need roots to fly
- Only passion gives meaning to reason
- It's only when you're lost that you can find your Self
- Power is light, control is heavy
- Love is the real bottom line
- Everyone holds a piece of the truth
- Wisdom knows nothing and honours everything
- Life is a virtual experience

Organisational wizards operate from a place of emergence and have both a strong sense of internal security and a deep faith in the Mystery. They're excited by life. Those with this leadership orientation do not see their primary identities defined by hierarchy or structure; they look at the contribution they can make to the organisation as a whole. These people engender great respect, investing their energy in creating a sense of organisational community in which others feel safe to take the risks needed to explore the deeper mysteries of life.

Such leaders focus on the interconnectedness of the disparate parts of the organisation, looking for opportunities to build synergy and cohesion. They create processes that weave the organisation together, in ways that support the unique identity of the different businesses and functions, and yet promote a sense of unity. These individuals make their decisions based on the bigger picture, encouraging others to do the same and to accept personal accountability for their choices.

To suggest that this is a simple task would be crazy. However, once enough people let go of the fundamental assumption of *survival of the fittest* and operate from the premise that if *somebody loses, nobody wins*, the creative force of the organisation will immediately shift. When a critical mass of people release the notion of scarcity and adopt the perception of abundance, everything changes! Leaving the space for mystery, magic and miracles.

The tremendous energy wasted in protecting scarce resources, drawing firm boundaries, competing internally and playing political games is then focused on lifting the spirit of the organisation to operate in environments of higher levels of complexity, setting the pace of change and promoting inspired performance.

The only way this can happen is for people to do the personal work necessary to free themselves from the fears and the self-limiting beliefs and behaviours that hold them back from expressing their authentic leadership power. From my experience, the primary function of leadership in any organisation today is to facilitate this process and to guide people to the edge of their own discovery. It is to inspire magic and miracles, and to illuminate the spiritual values that generate a contribution to humanity that people can take pride in. To share accountability, to learn from mistakes, to build strong cohesive networks and to actively invest in the evolution of consciousness, in an environment that encourages authentic expression of everything it means to be human – this is the new orientation to leadership. With this, performance excellence is a given.

Leadership Capabilities

- Respects all of life
- Builds community
- Has a sense of adventure
- Able to live with the unknown
- Takes time to be still
- Sees beyond boundaries
- Values the cycle of death and rebirth

Global Implications

No one knows the future, it's a blank canvas on which we are free to paint whatever picture we choose. We can paint in colours of war, peace, abundance, scarcity, love, fear, destruction or creation. The choice is up to each one of us as to how much of each colour we use. It is clear for all to see what we are choosing today and how it has brought us to a significant turning point in human history. Never before has the past become so obsolete, so fast.

The structures that provided security and separation are rapidly dissipating, as borders become inconsequential. The incredible power of the Internet is challenging every institutional norm, as it builds invisible bridges across political and national boundaries and unites the world. The uncertainty of tomorrow has never been so obvious as it is today, and it is becoming abundantly clear that few templates from the past will survive this revolution.

Rapid advances in technology are in danger of running ahead

of our ability as human beings to control their impact on our future. The main challenge is to ensure that the evolution of our consciousness keeps pace with the extraordinary 'progress' of every form of technology. The potential for catastrophic scenarios is so clear, and at this point no form of global governance or framework yet exists to promote the integration and security that could prevent it from happening. The external world is shifting its shape at a rapid rate. Until the majority of us deepen our understanding of human consciousness and the inner spiritual realms, it is unlikely that we will find the wisdom or moralistic code necessary to live in a world of such complexity.

Collective Consciousness

The Mystery holds the key to our future. All we have to do is be willing to enter it and be changed by what we learn if we are to avoid the potential global nightmares hanging over us. We will have to let go of much of what we believe we 'know' if we are to create a sustainable future. For example, love and compassion as they are popularly understood through religious teaching will not suffice if they continue to be rooted in egocentric and ethnocentric values.

The time is clearly here for us to come to some deeper spiritual understanding of our future as a human community. We have to encourage the awareness of our collective consciousness in order to balance the rapid development of technology. There is no denying the extent of the interdependencies that already exist and that are strengthening every moment. The issue is whether our consciousness can expand quickly enough to include the levels of complexity created by the vast differences in ideologies and values that exist throughout the world. Are we capable of operating from a mindset of alliance, breaking out of the patterns of our conditioning and honouring the power of the collective?

Paradoxically, such a change can only take place one person at a time. There are ways to increase the likelihood of such a transformation, and this is perhaps the most critical leadership task at this time. There are no past models of what it means to be 'worldcentric', and there are no 'quick fixes'. There are, however, plenty of sacred and philosophical tests that can open the doorway into the Mystery and reconnect us with the unity of our spiritual roots. Their wisdom is as relevant today as it has ever been. Buddhist teachings tell us that: 'we know we have arrived when we see every man as our brother and every woman as our sister.' Christianity tells us 'to love thy neighbour as thyself'. And yet what a challenge this is, when our externally motivated society distracts us from even knowing ourselves.

The Ultimate Challenge

The Seventh Key is perhaps the most challenging of all, because it opens the door that asks us to give up our attachment to everything and come home to ourselves. We have to find a faith that is deep enough to allow us to stand stripped of all ego identification in the place of not knowing, and discover who we really are. Only then can we reclaim our divine heritage and the unconditional love that is the source of our authentic power. With this consciousness we can truly love and serve others, and connect to a higher sense of being part of 'a universal family'. Our soul knows this to be true, and if we are to meet the challenges with which we are being confronted on both personal and global levels, then we all have work to do.

The whole thrust of our educational system needs to be deeply examined, with equal emphasis being placed on spiritual values and processes, so that children can learn to think for themselves and access their inner wisdom. The world's religions have to reconnect to their esoteric roots, where the values of love and unity are shared and where the notion of 'my God is better than your God' is simply absurd. Governments will have to find ways to participate in creating new forms of global governance promoting worldcentric thinking and behaviour.

This is a tremendously exciting time to be alive, and potentially terrifying if we allow greed and bigotry to take over. All of this is up to us. The collective picture only reflects the sum of our individual thinking. There is no value in continuing to believe that somebody else, somewhere else, is doing this to us. The first step in bringing about global transformation is the awareness that it is each one of us that is creating this reality. We do it through what we think, how we behave and the feelings we have about others and ourselves.

The framework of Seven Keys has been created to unlock the potential we all have to exercise leadership in the outer world. The text of this book is based on the assumption that the future of our world does not rest on the shoulders of a few, but in the hearts and minds of everyone. Each of the Keys accesses the energy needed to transcend the age-old issues of separation and connects us to the power of our authentic presence and our soul's authority.

To embark on this adventure takes tremendous courage, commitment, curiosity and compassion. It's a spiritual journey taking us through the darkness back to the light – bringing us home to the Mystery, with all that it means to be human. If we are to rediscover our unique destiny we have to learn to trust beyond understanding through a deepening of intimacy with others. This is the challenge that each of us faces as we expand our awareness and access our true leadership potential, accepting our role as co-creators of our global future. Sharing accountability for leadership in the *Relationship Age* is perhaps the most humbling and rewarding experience we will ever know.

Part Three

FOUR-DIMENSIONAL LEADERSHIP

FOUR-DIMENSIONAL LEADERSHIP

The number four provides the foundation upon
Which all things stand to sustain life.
Juno Jordan

THE JOURNEY THROUGH THE Seven Keys unlocks the potential we have to be fully alive on all four levels of existence, mind, body, spirit and emotion. Once we have released the energy held back in old patterns, we can refocus our lives in ways that support greater fulfilment. The consciousness we now bring to our daily living allows us to access our authentic leadership power as well as helping others to do the same.

If we are to go on growing, we have to remain aware of the process of change and renewal. It is easy to get caught out again by rigidly sticking to a new set of beliefs and assumptions that in turn become restrictive. Once we are able to see these 'soft structures' of the mind as facilitative, we can continuously adjust them accordingly as life unfolds. Alternatively we will become seduced by our own rhetoric. If we lose this perspective we will find ourselves recreating the imbalances that we have worked so hard to address. The Keys need to stay well oiled if they are to remain effective. We are all works in progress!

With economics, ecology and e-business only serving to heighten our awareness of our interconnectedness, the technical knowledge for which leaders used to be chosen is not enough to provide the inspirational leadership needed for the *Relationship Age*. Peter Senge talks about how 'We still think of "leaders" as people in control.' And yet many of us know only too well of the limitations of this orientation, and experience the consequences as the speed of change intensifies. Now is the time to step out with a new leadership consciousness that values and integrates all four dimensions of the human experience – mental, spiritual, emotional and physical.

The following provides a brief summary of these four energy dimensions and a framework for personal, organisational and global leadership that integrates all four levels of human existence. By looking at leadership holistically, this model supports the shift of consciousness necessary to operate with the alliance mindset.

The Four Dimensions

Mental

Our mind is the seat of our thoughts, assumptions, beliefs, attitudes, values and opinions. The mind influences how we see and experience the world. These experiences then either reinforce or challenge our existing patterns of thinking. If we are to take back the power to create our own lives, we need to examine the beliefs we hold and how they either help or hinder us in getting the results we want. For example, it would be very difficult for someone to take leadership and at the same time continue to believe that they are the victim of circumstances! If we are to take responsibility, we need to identify those assumptions and beliefs that might be holding us back, and work to transform them.

In the Seven Keys we explored the notion of how thought creates, and how what we hold in our mind tends to show up in our lives. What we focus on gets bigger! When we put energy into our fears they will gain power. When we put energy into our vision we will make it real. We have to consciously take control of our mind if we are to focus it in constructive and productive ways. If we allow our unconscious thinking patterns to run our lives we will find ourselves stuck in the ways of the past, unable to engage in processes of change and transformation.

How we think and what we think have tremendous power to create and destroy. As we become more aware of the soft structures of the mind – like our beliefs, and assumptions – we can more consciously choose the thoughts that serve us in creating the results we want to see in our own life and in the bigger world.

Spiritual

Spirit is the invisible force that brings vitality to life. When we are in touch with this dimension we find meaning and purpose in the universe. We have a sense of the broader context greater than our own individual existence, and are able to experience a deeper understanding of destiny. By acknowledging our role as co-creators, we intentionally focus our will in ways that serve a higher vision of humanity.

The spiritual dimension puts us in touch with a source of infinite energy that is benevolent and leads us to contribute in ways that promote greater levels of peace and harmony for all. We find ourselves seeing through the eyes of compassion, and opening our hearts to others, irrespective of their apparent origin. We see the oneness of everything and take accountability for our part of the whole.

We strengthen this dimension by remaining conscious of our motivation to be of service. If we overemphasise either self-interest or sacrifice, we will falter. Actively connecting to Spirit through prayer and meditation keeps us mindful of this energy and the power it has to nourish our lives.

Emotional

Emotions are essential to being human. They support us in building healthy connections in relationships in ways that allow intimacy and healing. Feelings are an important source of data and need to be honoured and respected if we are to be authentic in our expression. Often we get thoughts and feelings muddled up. We sometimes need others who are fluent in both the language and experience of emotion to help us to gain greater clarity of this dimension.

It is important to give voice to our feelings, so that we can make decisions that are good for us. Blocked emotional energy saps our strength. The less afraid we can be of our own and others feelings the more alive we will feel. This energy is also a powerful force in turning dreams into reality. It provides us with the power to act and to make our unique contribution. Without feeling, we will find ourselves lacking in enthusiasm for life, and only half-heartedly engaging in relationships.

Physical

We live in a world that places high value on physical action and the doing side of life! Nevertheless, we sometimes forget that we are responsible for ensuring that our bodies stay healthy. It is important to be aware of the lifestyle choices we make on a daily basis.

Unfortunately many of us have been educated not to worry about our health until it breaks down. In fact, we often push our bodies to the limit and then wonder why we get tired and ill. We have to learn to take care of our physical well-being in ways that allow us to remain physically vital for as long as we can.

We also have to learn to listen to the body's messages and not sacrifice our physical well-being to the mental and emotional demands that we (and too often others) place upon us. Often we don't heed the early warning signals that tell us we are running out of energy and getting close to burnout. We are all aware of the importance of our physical health in ensuring a fulfilling life. We just have to become more conscious of how to care for ourselves, and then take active steps to support this critical dimension of life.

Four New Leadership Archetypes

To take authentic leadership power, and to contribute the very best of who we are, involves paying attention to all four dimensions. Some of us have worked hard to develop some aspects, and paid less attention to others. If we want to achieve higher levels of fulfilment in our work and in our relationships, and make a worthwhile contribution in these changing times, then we will need to ensure that we are fully healthy in mind, body, spirit and emotions.

The following is a framework for a new orientation to leadership drawing on these four dimensions. It identifies four new

THE SEVEN KEYS AND THE FOUR DIMENSIONS

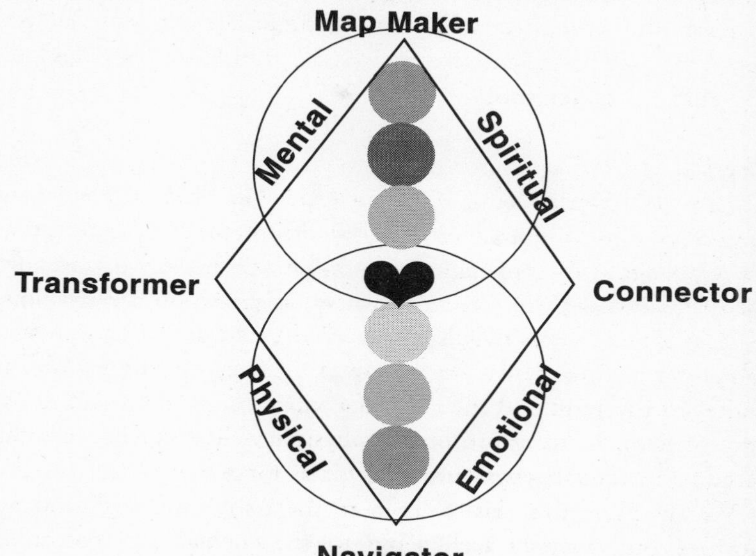

	THE TRANSFORMER	THE MAP MAKER	THE CONNECTOR	THE NAVIGATOR
Energy Dimensions	Mental & Physical	Mental & Spiritual	Spiritual & Emotional	Physical & Emotional
Core Quality	Courage	Curiosity	Compassion	Commitment
Role Focus	Creation & Destruction	Inspiration	Integration	Implementation
Key Relationship	Structure & Energy	Context & Meaning	Trust & Creativity	Vision & Action
Polarity	Stability & Change	Logic & Intuition	Doing & Being	Reactive & Creative
Primary Orientation	Thinker	Searcher	Healer	Doer
Contribution	Concept Builder	Vision Builder	Trust Builder	Thing Builder
Works with	Thoughts & Ideas	Dreams & Ideals	Feelings	Details
Develops	Intellect	Imagination	Caring	Concrete Skills
Believes in	Transformational Change	Infinite Possibility	Unconditional Love	Security
Time	Present Future	Future	Past Present Future	Present

leadership archetypes: the Transformer, the Map Maker, the Connector and the Navigator. To share the accountability for leadership in the twenty-first century we will each need access to all four of these. If we deny any one of them within ourselves, we will limit our potential to contribute.

We naturally have preferences for certain of these archetypal patterns over others. This will influence us to exhibit such preferences in a certain style, or styles of leadership in the outer world. For example, people may see us as Navigators and Transformers in our orientation to leadership. However, if we fail to draw on the Map Maker and Connector parts of ourselves in the overall functioning of our lives, we will be out of balance.

The Transformer

The Transformer deals primarily with mental and physical energies and creates concepts and processes that help us to make sense of the changing world. This is the part of ourselves that drives us to question and challenge our current realities, whether it is our jobs, where we live or our intellectual capabilities. It pushes us to stretch ourselves and to get us unstuck when our lives become too repetitive, or when we have outgrown our surroundings.

In providing leadership, Transformers help to define the desired state. They place a high value on logic and analysis and need to be more open to the sensitivities of people's feelings if they are to be successful. These people focus on all the Seven Keys, with a particular challenge of maintaining a healthy tension between the First Key, Establishing Security, and the Seventh Key, Honouring the Mystery. They focus the majority of their energy on task effectiveness, and do not invest heavily in the relationship side of the equation, leaving this to the Connector. Transformers love intellectual challenges and are excellent at testing out new ideas and setting strategic directions, especially if they involve the introduction of bold new concepts.

The core quality of the Transformer is Courage. It takes courage to change and to be willing to let go of the safety of the old. Unless we are able to release old thought forms and other kinds of physical structures that are holding us back, we will never have the energy to build new worlds. Whatever age we are, there is safety in the familiar and it is so easy to become complacent. Stepping out into what is new and untested takes considerable courage.

The inner Transformer is responsible for ensuring that the structures we create are serving our growth, whether they're the soft structures of the mind, like beliefs and assumptions, or the way we structure our lives and our organisations. This part of ourselves keeps us alert to the need for ongoing change.

The Transformer focuses on the relationship between energy and structure. If we allow outdated structures to channel our energy, we will stop growing and simply repeat the patterns of the past. When we challenge existing structures and break them down, it releases the energy we need to design and build new constructs that serve us better in today's reality.

One of the leadership tasks of Transformers is to shift the shape of organisational structures in order to ensure that the 'form' supports the strategic direction of the enterprise. This also helps to free the human energy trapped in old patterns of individual and organisational performance. Transformers are the agents of change.

When an organisation is lacking in this style of leadership, traditional behaviour is rewarded and risk takers are penalised. The compliance mindset is reinforced and there is an absence of organisational renewal. Transformers like to breakdown the barriers that inhibit growth and set a new and challenging direction.

In this respect the Transformer can be seen as both creator and destroyer. It is the part of us that challenges the status quo and asks us to let go of old habit patterns and behaviours, opening ourselves up to new possibilities. The inner Transformer prevents us from becoming complacent, takes us out of our comfort zone and leads us to achieve new levels of competence.

In a leadership role, Transformers are the visionaries, with a sharp intellect. They seek to create and resolve the tension between 'what is' and 'what could be'. These people are able to see a bigger picture, and are unafraid to challenge the established order. In fact that's their role! As a result they can sometimes find themselves out in the cold, or 'getting shot' metaphorically, or even actually, if they become too threatening.

The challenge of the Transformer is managing the polarity of stability and change. If this part of us is overactive, we find ourselves in a permanent process of transition, never feeling a sense of belonging. Without a certain amount of structure to support us, we find it difficult to focus and our energies become diffused. We see this in people who are always on the move and who are afraid to settle down.

When our inner Transformer is asleep, we are likely to fear and resist change. We bury our head in the sand and hope things will blow over. We can end up 'stuck in a rut' repeating the same old stories and failing to open our minds to new ideas and concepts.

Transformers are dynamic and take the initiative to make change happen. Once the ball is rolling they sometimes lose interest and seek out new and different challenges in which to invest their intellectual capabilities. In an organisational context, if they fail to manage the polarity of stability and change, these people can be a disturbing force, never providing focus for long enough to get the energy channelled in a productive direction.

Transformers often hook into whatever concept is the 'flavour of the month' and find themselves unable to create sustainable change. In order to be effective, they need to value both ends of the polarity, and to become more conscious of their own and others' feelings. When they do, they can be charismatic leaders who provide the inspiration and the direction for people to grow and achieve.

The Map Maker

The Map Maker works with both mental and spiritual energies. It is the part of us that is responsible for challenging us to deepen our awareness of 'what is', reminding us to look for more than what meets the eye in order to understand reality. When our Map Maker is in the driver's seat, we are likely to find ourselves seeing through a very different lens. We become aware that it is not only the physical world that provides stability. There is also an invisible web of intricate threads weaving us together in relationships of interdependency.

Map Makers work predominantly with the upper Four Keys – Honouring the Mystery, Trusting Intuition, Voicing Truth and Inspiring Love. These people naturally promote balance between task and relationship. Their biggest challenge is not to get 'lost in the clouds'. They have to work hard to ensure that their insights are grounded in reality. Finding a Navigator to act as an 'anchor' can be a tremendous asset.

The core quality of the Map Maker is curiosity. It's the voice within us that asks us to explore unseen worlds and to create new 'maps' to make sense of a bigger universe. It drives us beyond the physical reality into those realms where all things are possible. Map Makers are the dreamers, the innovators, the spiritual teachers and the lantern-bearers.

Curiosity is a great asset that many of us shut down as we grow up. The compliance mindset does not encourage the development of this quality. The old adage that 'curiosity killed the cat' rings in the ears of most of us brought up with a traditional education. In environments that are changing so fast, we must learn to open our minds to new possibilities and to explore beyond the edges of the known world. The potential we have, intellectually and spiritually, appears limitless. Engaging our inner Map Maker prepares us to venture into uncharted territory.

The Map Maker focuses on the relationship between context and meaning. This is the part of us that is responsible for ensuring that our lives are purposeful and that our values are consistent with a higher intention. Today, many of us are seeking greater meaning in our lives, and are finding it difficult to make sense of the chaos and the confusion that surrounds us.

Map Makers create new frameworks of understanding, elevating our perspective so that we can view the current reality through a 'higher' lens. They help us to sit in the helicopter and to see things through 'new eyes'. This is the part of us that seeks to understand rather than to judge.

Our inner Map Makers often 'speak' to us through symbols.

We become aware of a language that our left-brain finds hard to understand because it is based more on intuition than on logic. Symbolic language includes music, numbers, colours and vibration. Map Makers teach us that there is no such thing as coincidence – everything has meaning once you expand the context.

As a leadership style, the Map Maker creates alternative scenarios in which the Transformers can set the strategy. They connect to higher sources of inspiration to broaden the context, using data that is both concrete and abstract. Without something to inspire us, life can often appear meaningless if we are unable to connect to a bigger purpose.

In organisations, Map Makers use their wisdom and their intellect to inspire others to reach beyond the established boundaries in ways that serve the evolution of the whole enterprise. In leadership roles, they are often inspirational speakers and communicate spiritual values and concepts in ways that are understandable and encourage people to take the risks needed to change. Like Transformers, they can be charismatic. The difference lies in the nature of their energy. Whereas Transformers tend to be more dynamic, asserting themselves by initiating change, the energy of Map Makers is more magnetic. People are drawn to them and find a richness of spiritual wisdom and insight that allows them to release attachment to the past.

The challenge of the Map Maker is to manage the polarity of intuition and logic. Their success depends on their ability to translate intuitive data into something that is understandable within a logical framework. Much of the creativity and expansiveness of Map Makers comes from their ability to suspend logic and enter unknown realms, collecting new information in symbolic ways. If they get lost in these alternative realities, it is hard for them to share their findings in ways that have relevance.

Map Makers have the capacity to bridge the spiritual and corporeal worlds. They are able to interpret abstract images into concrete ideas that are usable in the world of form. Without the Map Maker, the world would soon become mundane and repetitive, lacking in meaning. Many organisations are suffering through an absence of these people. It won't be until intuition is put on a par with reason in institutional settings that the enthusiasm and expansiveness that Map Makers inspire will be truly valued.

The Connector

The Connector works primarily with spiritual and emotional energies. This is the part of us that is the weaver, connecting the many parts of ourselves so that we can experience the full potential of our creativity. The Connector allows us to identify the unique gifts we have to bring to the world, and to learn to trust ourselves enough to express them. It helps strengthen our self-esteem, and to identify old wounds that need healing so that we can find happiness and fulfilment.

Connectors help organisations with the human side of change. They encourage the expression of emotions in ways that keep the energy moving, allowing people to face their fears and release the past. Our inner Connector helps to free us from patterns that are self-defeating and that cause us to be cynical, despairing, guilt-ridden or shameful. It's the part of us that leads us into the land of 'faith and freedom' where we can make healthy and self-supporting choices.

Connectors work with all Seven Keys, focusing on the development of healthy relationships. These people teach us how to integrate our feelings and express them in constructive ways. Like Map Makers, Connectors work with less tangible forces and are invaluable in helping to free up the energy blockages that prevent people from performing at their highest level. They need the help of Transformers to focus the emotional and spiritual energies into task-related activities.

The core quality of the Connector is compassion. Before we can truly have compassion for others we must first find compassion within ourselves, for ourselves and for our own suffering. There is probably no one alive today who has not suffered at some time. Most of us need more access to our inner Connectors to make sense of that suffering and to come to terms with the pain that we feel.

When the Connector is overly strong it is likely that we are working either to resolve emotional wounds left over from childhood or from more recent experiences that have left us 'off centre'. At times like this we need to find someone with a compassionate heart, so that we can express ourselves without fear of judgement. Connectors provide us with a safe space to reveal our vulnerabilities and deepen our self-understanding.

The Connector focuses on the relationship between trust and creativity. It is difficult to access our creative potential if we do not know, or trust ourselves, on all four levels of existence. With a lack of value placed on feelings, many of us have repressed emotions. If we are fortunate, these bubble to the surface and demand attention.

We may become more emotionally aware as a result of a physical illness or as a result of stresses in our personal or professional lives. Changes in relationships or specific incidents can also be the catalysts for emotional reawakening. Whatever the trigger, we find ourselves wanting to heal and move on, knowing that emotional baggage is a heavy burden that holds us back from our experience of life. It is the Connector who works with us to deepen our levels of intimacy (into me see), so that we can be more authentic and trusting of ourselves and of others, in relationships.

There is a clear connection between trust and creativity. In organisations where there is little trust, there is little creativity. The Connector's role is to legitimise the language of emotion in the working environment in order to release the potential people have to make a contribution. They provide safe spaces where people are unafraid to express their innate creativity and experience the more emotional parts of themselves, without risk or fear of consequences.

With change becoming a way of life, the acknowledgement of feelings becomes a critical component of an organisation's success. Placing a higher value on this leadership style will only serve to increase overall effectiveness at times of transformation. Failure to do so will limit the energy available to invest in the growth of the enterprise.

Connectors work across boundaries, strengthening relationships and helping create strong networks and support systems that encourage growth and development. They are invaluable at times of mergers and acquisitions where two or more cultures are coming together and where there's a need for optimal performance from all players. A lot of our learning processes cause us to focus on separation rather than connection, and this can be costly and draining to the energy of an organisation. When we look at the pieces and the parts rather than seeing the dynamic whole, we lose a lot of the potential for creative synergies.

Connectors look through a holistic lens, seeing things as integrated, woven together and connected. They see how everything is part of a larger pattern, and focus on the common ground on which we stand and the common bonds that link us together as humanity. They believe in people-centred leadership, and are the team builders and the networkers, integrating the disparate parts into something that is cohesive and flowing. Fortunately for us, there is increasing awareness of the need for this leadership orientation in organisational settings.

Many Connectors, however, are still not integrated into the mainstream, and often play a marginal role. Not having enough of them 'out in the open' accounts for some of the absence of trust and risk-taking. Without an understanding of the value of emotional authenticity in relationships, people feel a sense of isolation and disconnection. They are unwilling to put themselves on the line, concerned about what may happen if they do.

Some of the more progressive organisations are placing a higher value on this leadership style, often as a result of painful downsizing processes (or mergers and acquisitions). Others are just becoming aware of the real value of interconnection and the need to build the competencies to encourage high-quality relationships. Mentoring programs and a stronger focus on coaching are helping to legitimise the role of the Connector.

Consultants and some human-resource professionals often model this leadership style. They look for ways to integrate the separate parts of an organisation to leverage the whole in the service of the 'customer'. However, until the level of what Goleman refers to as 'Emotional Intelligence' increases, it is a role that is unlikely to become mainstream in established institutions.

In the broader community, Connectors are becoming more abundant. This is enabling people to find the support needed to explore the deeper emotional issues that cause much of their physical stress. In this way they are able to heal old wounds and free up the energy and move on.

Connectors are exquisite listeners and are usually extremely intuitive. They draw on the spiritual dimension to guide them through the complex sea of emotions.

Connectors get a great deal of satisfaction from developing people and in helping them deepen their sense of self-worth. For Connectors to be fully effective in their leadership roles they need to manage the polarity between 'being and doing'.

Traditional organisations often look upon these people as 'average' performers, because the results of their work are not always tangible. The 'soft skills' that Connectors possess in abundance are difficult to measure and not always obvious to the bottom line. Most of us have been educated to emphasise the doing end of the polarity and need help to place a higher value on 'beingness'.

The challenge of the Connector is to support us in harmonising these polarities so that we make even greater contributions through our ability to develop high-quality relationships. If we fail to take time to focus on the 'softer side' of life, we lose some of the richness that comes from forming quality connections with others. Organisations that drive their people relentlessly will find lowering levels of trust and creativity. The Connector's role in this changing environment is to redress this imbalance and free the extraordinary creative potential that is still hidden in the shadows of some of the world's most exciting enterprises.

The Navigator

The Navigator works with physical and emotional energies and helps us to realise our vision in the concrete world of day-to-day life. It is the part that leads us to act. The Navigator wants us to get our hands dirty, feeling the soil between our fingers. It helps us to take risks, deal with practical realities and see things as they 'really' are. It guides us through the 'real world', ensuring that our actions are consistent with our visions, and that we do the 'doing' necessary to make our dreams come true.

People who have the Navigator predominant in their lives are almost always 'busy'. They don't tend to sit still for long and are very much in touch with 'reality' as they live very much in the present. They are pragmatic, matter-of-fact people in their approaches, and are those who call a spade a spade! They step firmly on the ground and are unafraid to make decisions leading to action and results. In organisations they are the trouble-shooters and the fire-fighters, guiding us through the problems we encounter as we turn abstract ideas into concrete form.

Navigators focus primarily on the first Four Keys, Establishing Security, Generating Passion, Sharing Power and Inspiring Love. They work effectively with both task and relationship, and are able to engage people in activities that provide a sense of achievement. Navigators like tangible results and are both practical and caring. They need to connect to the Map Maker from time to time, to ensure that their contribution is aligned with a higher purpose. Otherwise they can use a lot of energy achieving results that add little overall value.

The core quality of this aspect of leadership consciousness is commitment. For us to really engage fully in life, we need to make clear commitments, to live in present time and to contribute in ways that make a difference. If we don't, we are likely to find ourselves ungrounded in the physical world, never really feeling at home on the planet, and unable to achieve our potential as full human beings.

Making commitments is a bold step for many people who find comfort in simply exploring theories and possibilities. Until we do, it is unlikely that we will know the incredible sense of achievement that comes from making things happen. Our inner Navigator asks us to commit ourselves to action and to become fully involved in the human race. It pushes us to take a stand for what we believe in and to demonstrate this through action. Without commitment it is hard to feel secure and to experience the sense of rooting necessary to achieve and grow.

The Navigator focuses on the relationship between vision and action. This is the part of us that 'makes real' the dreams and ideas that we have imagined, and brings us to where the rubber meets the road. We can create wonderful concepts, generate alternative scenarios, free up our emotional energy, but without implementation in the real world any act of creation is incomplete.

When Navigators remember to lift their eyes upward to the stars, to ensure their action is in alignment with the vision, they can generate tremendous excitement. Their 'can do' conviction is a strong motivational force, and with clear measures of success, people feel a wonderful sense of achievement. However, we can all imagine the consequences if people are following this leadership orientation unaware of the changing realities. They are simply repeating the past, busy doing what they've always done.

Navigators are masterful at implementation. They are passionate about results and arriving successfully at their destination! They focus on what needs to be done and how to do it. In organisations these people hold only brief meetings to ensure that everyone is actively involved in the task or project, and that roles and expectations are clear. They find endless conversations on the bigger picture tedious and time-wasting. Navigators are the classic example of the Nike slogan, 'Just Do It!'

These people learn by doing, not reflecting or even planning, just gathering people together and getting on with it. Given a challenging task with a clear result, these people are in their element. We need them to get us where we want to go. Navigators are the builders, they pour the concrete and they lay the bricks! In organisations they sell the product, care for their customers and set performance targets that will challenge them to achieve. They have little tolerance for people who are out of touch with reality and who spend too much time locked up in their ivory towers.

One of the greatest challenges the Navigator faces is managing 'the reactive and creative' polarity. If you take a look at these two words you will notice that the words are anagrams of each other. The only difference between them is where you place the 'C'! With this in mind, think about the letter 'C' as meaning 'see'. Now we can look at them a little differently and recognise that when we are being reaCtive we tend to 'see' in the middle of things, and when we are being Creative we 'see' up front!

The word active can be found in both! This is what Navigators care most about, and as long as they're busy that's all that matters. If they go to sleep, and lose touch with the creative end of the polarity, they can find themselves constantly in reaction to what is going on around them. As long as they are engaged in activity they don't always stop to see whether or not it is productive. Of course when short-term survival issues are at stake, the reactive orientation is very important. The difficulty comes when it is the unconscious default position.

Focusing only on the creative end also has its downside. If we're busy driving along gazing at the stars, we may find ourselves going off the road. Organisations with this leadership style predominant need to ensure that their Navigators are holding a healthy tension between these polarities. They are then in a position to set their own standards of performance and to see obstacles as challenges to test their resolve. Navigators are happy to draw on proven processes and are unafraid to find a new and different solution if necessary. They will rarely waste valuable energy simply reinventing the wheel.

In organisations, we have many potential twenty-first-century Navigators. A lot of them are still using outdated intellectual 'equipment'! They are continuing to operate in the ways of the past driving for results without a clear sense of a bigger vision in a broader context, connected to a higher intention. This is why it is the combination and integration of all four of these leadership archetypes, both in our inner worlds as well as our outer realities, that is essential to our future well-being and our sustainability as a global society.

14 □

LEADING WITH INTENTION

Outside all notions of right and wrong there is a field,
will you meet me there?
Rumi

AS WE MOVE MORE fully into the *Relationship Age*, we need Transformers, Map Makers, Connectors and Navigators if we are to create a new orientation to leadership that values diversity and promotes sustainability. Naturally each one of us will favour some orientations over others. It is important that we are, first, aware of our preferences and, second, conscious of those aspects that may remain underdeveloped. Most of us have work to do if we are to make our full contribution.

There is however a fifth dimension – the soul – that allows the alignment of mind, body, spirit and emotion in the service of a greater purpose. Our Soul's Intention is the 'Master Key' that gives our life meaning and focus – it is the final piece in the puzzle.

The Fifth Dimension

The word 'soul' is used throughout this book without any single definition. One way of understanding its role is to see it as the fifth dimension, adding to mind, body, spirit and emotion and, paradoxically, integrating all of them in a way that allows us to be 'at one' with ourselves. The soul is the essence or core of our being, bringing purpose and meaning to our life. Each soul arrives on the planet with a 'learning contract'. The ego's function is to be its partner in a process of growth and development as we fulfil our destiny.

When we talk about growing – beyond the physical notions of

the word – it is usually the soul's growth to which we refer. The soul is that part of us that seeks to deepen our understanding of our true potential and the infinite possibilities open to all of us. Denise Breton and Christopher Largent tell us that the 'Soul is our guiding center, our touchstone for what feels right in life and what's ours to do. Soul is our reason for coming here as well as our reason for staying. Soul tells us about us – not as others want, expect, or imagine us to be, but as we are in our innermost being.'

Much of our Western education leads us to lose touch with the feelings of unity that come from a connection with our soul's guidance. We learn instead to follow the needs of our ego, taking us into a world of duality and separation. Most of us at some point in our life deeply feel this sense of loss. We ask: Why are we here? What's life all about? Who am I really? Many of us at this point start what is described as 'soul-searching'. We are literally looking to rediscover our own soul, and reclaim the meaning of our life. If we are unable to reconnect to this deeper intention we become 'lost and lonely souls'.

Our souls exist outside of time and space; they have no gender, no race and no religion. The personality is temporal. It is what the soul dresses up in to learn its lessons. In true partnership, ego and soul are a dynamite combination with limitless creative potential to grow and contribute. Together they allow us to experience both our humanity and our divinity in the expression of our life. When we free up the energy of 'the Seven Keys' we make the commitment to clear up all the misconceptions and fears we have about who we are and why we are here. We find that behind any facade our ego has built to protect us lies our authentic self and the tremendous potential we have to contribute.

This journey of soul discovery challenges us to let go of being overly attached to our ego's needs, bringing us to the place within ourselves where we reconnect to a higher intention and reclaim our soul's authority. Once we consciously connect to this inner guidance, our energy changes and our whole perspective on life is very different. We experience our relationship with everything and everyone in new and sacred ways. There's a sense of liberation and of unity; of unconditional love and respect for the courage it takes to be human. We feel a deep desire to make our unique contribution in the service of the whole. Our fundamental motivation for living becomes clearer as our awareness expands and we connect to our 'soul's intention'. It is this connection that provides us with the Master Key to our authentic leadership power, and to being at ease in a world of polarity and paradox.

The Master Key

We live in a world that is full of contradictions. The experience of duality is part of our human nature and the source of many of the fears we face in our search to live fulfilling lives. How we manage the tension this creates, is at the core of claiming the power of our authentic presence and promoting a new orientation to leadership. Once we claim our soul's authority, speaking with a voice that integrates all the dimensions, we move from simply living within tension – to living with intention!

The understanding of polarity and paradox is one of the soul's many gifts. It is also the platform for the new leadership consciousness. The core assumption of the alliance mindset, 'if somebody loses, nobody wins', suggests that the doorway to unity opens once we learn to honour our inherent diversity. Once we accept that we are separate unique individuals, we paradoxically find that we are all one.

When we are clear of our soul's intention we learn to live with paradox and to look at polarity through a new lens. Instead of feeling conflicted by the tension of opposites, like right and wrong; doing and being; security and freedom; past and future, we learn to accept the inherent paradox. We recognise the dynamic energy that connects both ends of the polarity and are able to see how they serve the whole.

Lao Tsu says in the *Tao Te Ching*:

> *Under heaven all can see beauty as beauty only because there is ugliness.*
> *All can know good as good only because there is evil.*

Therefore having and not having arise together.
Difficult and easy complement each other.
Long and short contrast each other;
High and low rest upon each other;
Voice and sound harmonise each other;
Front and back follow each other.

When our ego is in charge we find ourselves wanting to resolve the tension between two polarities and to establish balance – something that we will rarely achieve except for moments. We've all experienced examples of this in everyday life. One of the most common New Year's resolutions is to find a better balance between work and play. But what tends to happen is that we focus on the pole that is out of sync. Soon the other end of the polarity demands our attention and we switch our focus accordingly in our attempt to find balance.

Balance as a goal has little real value because it is a static state and fails to take into account the dynamic energy that exists between all polarities. Without a higher intention there is nothing to determine the appropriate energy flow between the poles and we get trapped in the tension of opposites, becoming frustrated at our inability to create a balanced life! From the soul's perspective the flow of energy between the poles is not seen as a seesaw, or as scales that need to be balanced; rather, it is represented by the symbol of infinity, with energy flowing constantly between the polarities in the service of a higher intention. Once we see duality through new eyes we achieve a quality of peace that the ego alone cannot provide.

In organisations that allow the structure to drive their strategies we see this dynamic played out in many ways. When there is an absence of a bigger picture that makes the choices obvious, huge amounts of management time gets consumed in people becoming polarised around issues like short-term costs and long-term investment, centralisation and decentralisation, internal and external focus, taking risks and playing it safe. It is only when the leadership of these institutions connect to the higher intention of

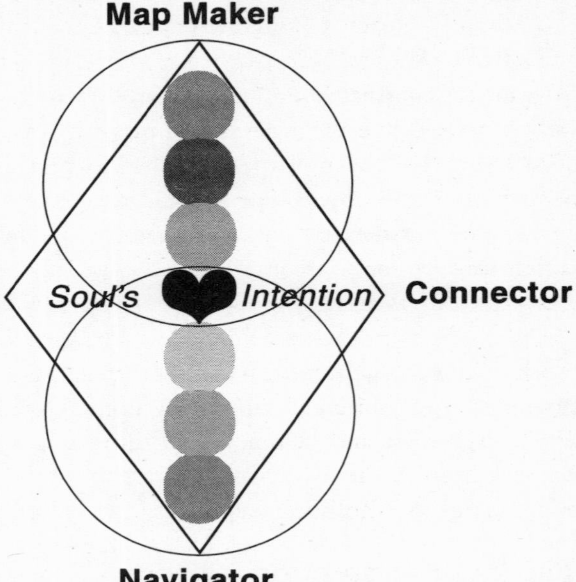
THE FIFTH DIMENSION
Map Maker
Transformer
Soul's
Intention
Connector
Navigator

LIVING WITHIN TENSION

LIVING WITH INTENTION

their enterprises, allowing this to determine the structure and processes, that they will find they are fulfilling their true function.

When we reach a point where there is no need to make one end of the polarity right or wrong, we can then hold them in a dynamic tension that allows both to have potency. From this position we can experience the true power inherent in paradox without a need to resolve the pull of the poles. To gain this awareness, we have to align the power of our authentic presence with our soul's intention.

Instead of being torn apart by the pull of the poles, we learn to accept 'this swinging rhythm . . .' and open what the philosopher Cyprian Smith refers to as the 'Wisdom Eye or the Eye of the Heart'. From this perspective we 'see that these contraries are all contained finally in an all-embracing unity; God and Man, pleasure and pain, success and failure, are all ultimately one in God.' Once we see through the Eye of the Heart, we look at the notion of opposites from a holistic perspective.

The Soul's Intention

By opening the Wisdom Eye we connect with the deeper meaning of our lives and rediscover our soul's intention. We then provide leadership in ways that are supportive of greater harmony in a global society. We no longer see life only in shades of black or white, but as a colourful tapestry. We start to look at things in terms of their relatedness, and focus on the complementary nature of 'apparent' opposites. We discover how we can allow the different aspects to co-exist and support growth, at the same time as being unafraid to make the tough choices. The value of paradox and polarity from the soul's perspective is then to stretch our minds to new awarenesses and to free us from the limitations of our current thinking. This shift to a higher viewpoint where polarity and paradox are valued is one of the basic building blocks of the alliance mindset and at the heart of authentic leadership.

To gain greater clarity of our soul's intention all we need to do is to ask these simple questions:

- What are my greatest strengths?
- What am I learning?
- What am I doing that serves the bigger picture?
- How do I support the growth of others?
- What is my heart's desire?

As we explore these questions we arrive at a place within ourselves where we – **I**gnite **N**ow **T**he **E**nergy **N**eeded **T**o **I**nspire **O**ur **N**obility. We free the power of our authentic presence and claim our leadership role. Our soul's intention gives our life dignity. It strengthens the spiritual and moral awareness needed to make our unique contribution to the world in every moment. We take our place 'at the table' and are unafraid to state the truth of what we know to be so. We align all the energies of mind, body, spirit and emotions, with a unified reason for being, and discover the magic that happens when we accept our role as co-creators.

When our intention is clear we find that we can focus our energy in the present, in potent ways. When our soul's authority directs it, we bring a force for change that is inspired by a higher knowing allowing us to use our will in the service of others. We learn to live in the here and now with the Seven Keys in the unlocked position. It is an incredible experience and we know without a shadow of a doubt that we are here for a reason.

Deep down we all know how to access our soul's intention. The knowledge has been there since the beginning of our life. Plato talks about how our soul crosses the 'River of Forgetting' before we take on human form. We lose the conscious memory of the intention of this life so that we can learn our lessons and remember why we're here. Our journey through time and space gives us the opportunity to unlock the potential we each have for fulfilling that higher intention. As we engage in this 'process of remembering' we reclaim the power of our authentic presence. We let go of the need to define ourselves solely by the material and physical world and reconnect to our spiritual heritage, the source of our true leadership potential.

In remembering, we heal the wounds of separation that have brought so much conflict and pain. We are able to see the world in a different way, one which allows us to be a part of it and apart from it. We take on the role of the witness and act from a place of discernment without any attachment to outcome. The decisions we make are neither right nor wrong they are simply choices that have consequences. As Professor Albus Dumbledore tells Harry Potter in J.K. Rowling's *Chamber of Secrets*, 'It is our choices, Harry, that show what we truly are, far more than our abilities.' It is this power of choice that allows us to stand in the centre at the still-point and consciously determine what combination of the four leadership roles of Transformer, Map Maker, Connector and Navigator best serves at any given moment of time.

Once we commit to lives of conscious choice guided by our soul's intention, and unlock the energy of the Seven Keys, we come home to ourselves. It is an awesome commitment that challenges us to fundamentally shift our ground of being and free ourselves from any beliefs that may have kept us comfortable in our complacency. We have to confront all the fears and insecurities that hold us back from claiming the power of our authentic leadership.

The reward in doing so is that we touch the wellspring of unconditional love and reconnect to a higher intelligence that reminds us of our 'oneness' with everything. We join with others in relationships of authenticity, with a spirit of cooperation. We take responsibility for the condition of our lives, and share accountability for the state of our world. We know in our hearts that transformation is an inside job and that we are each here for a purpose. With this awareness, we come face to face with a new paradox – leadership in a global society is a very personal matter!

Love All, Serve All
Sai Baba

REFERENCES AND FURTHER READING

Adams, John D. *Transforming Leadership* (2nd ed.). Alexandria VA: Miles River Press, 1998.

——. *Thinking Today as if Tomorrow Mattered: The Rise of a Sustainable Consciousness*. San Francisco, CA: Eartheart, 2000

Arewa, Caroline Shola. *Opening the Spirit*. London: Thorsons, 1998.

Arrien, Angeles PhD. *The Four-Fold Way*. San Francisco: HarperSanFrancisco, 1993.

Autry, James. *Love and Profit: The Art of Caring Leadership*, New York: William Morrow, 1991.

Bach, Richard. *Illusions: The Adventures of a Reluctant Messiah*. London: Arrow Books, 1998.

Barrentine, Pat, ed. *When the Canary Stops Singing*. San Francisco, CA: Berrett-Koehler, 1993.

Bohm, David. *Wholeness and the Implicate Order*. London and New York: Art Paperbacks, 1980.

——. *On Dialogue*. Ojai, CA: David Bohm Seminars, 1990.

Breton, Denise and Largent, Christopher. *Love, Soul and Freedom: Dancing with Rumi on the Mystic Path*. Minnesota: Hazelden, 1998.

Business Week, 11 May 1992, pp. 65–75; 26 April 1993, pp. 56–79

Byron, Katie, *Loving What Is*. London: Rider, 2000.

Chopra, Deepak. *How To Know God: The Soul's Journey Into The Mystery of Mysteries*. London: Rider, 2000.

Covey, Stephen R. *Principle-Centered Leadership*. New York: Simon and Schuster, 1992.

——. *The Seven Habits of Highly Effective People: Powerful Lessons in Personal Change*. New York: Simon and Schuster, 1993.

Dalai Lama. *The Dalai Lama's Book of Wisdom*. London: Thorsons, 1999.

Dyer, Wayne W. *You'll See It When You Believe It*. New York: Morrow and Company Inc., 1989.

Fritz, Robert. *Principles for Creating What You Want To Create: The Path of Least Resistance*. Salem, MA: DMA, 1984.

Gawain, Shakti. *The Four Levels of Healing*. Mill Valley, CA: Nataraj, 1997.

Geller, Uri and Appleton, Lulu. *Mind Medicine: The Secret of Powerful Healing*. Shaftesbury, Dorset: Element Books, 1999.

Gerber, Richard MD. *Vibrational Medicine: New Choices for Healing Ourselves*. Santa Fe, NM: Bear and Company, 1988.

Gibran, Kahlil. *The Prophet*. London: William Heinemann, 1988.

Goleman, Daniel. *Emotional Intelligence*. London: Bloomsbury, 1996.

——. *The New Leaders*. London: Little, Brown, 2002.

Hanh, Thich Nhat. *Peace is Every Step*. New York: Bantam Books, 1991.

Handy, Charles. *The Age of Unreason*. Boston: Harvard Business School Press, 1990.

Harman, Willis, PhD. *Global Mind Change: The Promise of the Last Years of the Twentieth Century*. Indianapolis: Knowledge Systems, 1998.

Hawley, Jack. *Rewakening the Meaning of Work*. San Francisco, CA: Berrett-Koehler, 1993.

Hillman, James. *The Soul's Code: In Search of Character and Calling*. New York: Warner Books, 1996.

His Holiness the Dalai Lama and Cutler, Howard C, MD. *The Art of Happiness: A Handbook for Living*. New York: Riverhead Books, 1998.

Judith, Anodea PhD. *Wheels of Life: A User's Guide to the Chakra System*. Minnesota: Llewellyn Publications, 1999.

Lao Tsu (trans. Gia-Fu Feng and Jane English). *Tao Te Ching*. London: Wildwood House, 1980.

Laszlo, Ervin, Grof, Stanislav, and Russell, Peter. *The Consciousness Revolution*. Shaftesbury, Dorset: Element, 1999.

Leadbeater, C. W. *The Chakras*. Madras, India: Quest Books, 1927.

Leider, Richard and Shapiro, David. *Repacking Your Bags: Lighten Your Load For The Rest of Your Life*. San Francisco, CA: Berrett-Koehler, 1995.

Marie Claire (UK Edition,) February 2003, pp. 93–4 Regan, Katy and Hanabeth Luke. My Boyfriend Died in Bali – I Escaped

Moore, Thomas. *Care of the Soul*. New York: Harper Perennial, 1992.

Myss, Caroline, PhD. *Anatomy of the Spirit: The Seven Stages of Power and Healing*. New York: Three Rivers Press, 1996.

Neihardt, John G. *Black Elk Speaks*. New York: Washington Square Press, 1972.

Nouwen, Henri J.M. *The Inner Voice of Love: A Journey Through Anguish to Freedom*. London: Darton, Longman and Todd 1999.

Ozaniec, Naomi. *The Elements of the Chakras*. Shaftesbury, Dorset: Element Books, 1990.

Parsons, Rob. *The Heart of Success: Making it in Business without Losing it in Life*. London: Hodder & Stoughton, 2002.

Paulus, Trina. *Hope for The Flowers*. New York: Paulist Press, 1972.

Perspectives, Volume 12, Number 4, December 1998. World Business Academy.

Pinkola Estes, Clarissa. *Women Who Run With the Wolves: Contacting the Power of The Wild Woman*. London: Rider, 1997.

Quinn, Daniel. *Ishmael: An Adventure of Mind and Spirit*. London: Hodder & Stoughton, 1992.

Ray, Michael and Rinzler, Alan (eds). *The New Paradigm in Business*. Los Angeles: Jeremy P. Tarcher, 1993.

Renesch, John and Defoore, Bill (eds). *The New Bottom Line: Bringing Heart & Soul to Business*. San Francisco, CA: Sterling & Stone, 1996.

Ruiz, Don Miguel. *The Four Agreements: A Practical Guide to Personal Freedom*. San Rafael, CA: Amber-Allen Publishing, 1997.

——. *The Mastery of Love: A Practical Guide to the Art of Relationship*. San Rafael, CA: Amber-Allen Publishing, 1997.

Russell, Peter. *Waking up in Time*. San Francisco, CA: Harper, 1996.

Saint-Exupéry, Antoine de. *The Little Prince*. London: Mammoth, 1991.

Scherer, John and Shook, Larry. *Work and the Human Spirit*. Spokane, WA: JS & A, 1993.

Schulz, Mona Lisa MD, PhD. *Awakening Intuition*. London: Bantam Books, 1999.

Senge, Peter M. *The Fifth Discipline*. London: Random House, 1999.

Shine, Betty. *Cosmic Colour*. London: HarperCollins, 2000.

Smith, Cyprian, *Spiritual Life as Taught by Meister Eckhart: The Way of the Paradox*. London: Darton, Longman & Todd, 1996.

Spencer, Sabina. *Reflections*. New York: Vantage Press, 1987.

Spencer, Sabina and John D. Adams. *Life Changes: the Seven Stages of Personal Growth*. New York: Paraview, 2002.

Stone, Hal PhD and Stone, Sidra PhD. *Embracing Our Selves: The Voice Dialogue Manual*. Mill Valley, CA: Nataraj, 1996.

Vaughan, Frances E. *Shadows of the Sacred: Seeing through Spiritual Illusions*. Wheaton, IL: Quest Books, 1995.

Walsch, Neale Donald. *Conversations with God: An Uncommon Dialogue*. Books 1, 2 & 3 New York: G. P. Putnam's Sons, 1996–1999.

Walsh, Roger MD, PhD. *The 7 Central Practices to Awaken Heart and Mind: Essential Spirituality*. New York: John Wiley and Sons, 1999.

Welwood, John PhD. *Journey of the Heart*. New York: Harper Perennial, 1991.

Wilber, Ken. *A Brief History of Everything*. Boston: Shambala Publications, 1993.

Wheatley, Margaret J. *Leadership and the New Science: Discovering Order in a Chaotic World*. San Francisco: Berrett-Koehler, 1999.

White, Eagle. *The Path of the Soul*. Oxford: The University Press, 1987.

Zukav, Gary. *The Seat of the Soul: An Inspiring Vision of Humanity's Spiritual Destiny*. London: Rider, 1991.

Zukav, Gary and Francis, Linda. *The Heart of the Soul: Emotional Awareness*. New York: Fireside, 2002.

ACKNOWLEDGEMENTS

THERE ARE SO MANY people to whom I am grateful, that to name them all would take a book in itself! There are some of you who I would especially like to acknowledge for the contribution you have made to my life. In sharing time with each of you, I am the richer for it, and so too is this book.

I would like to thank my friends and 'family' in Europe, for their loving support and encouragement, Michael & Laura Andrae, Pamela Allsop, Rebecca Andrew, Alessio & Marissa Arcando, Laura Atkins, Jonathan Bailey, Svetlana Balanova, Urban & Karin Berggren, David Brown, Gareth Brown, Julie Conner, Alan & Hilary Davidson, Denise Delaney, Eckart Dissen, Jeroen Drontmann, Jo Dunbar, Adrian Dunford, Stig Eriksson, Sue Frisby, Ben Gieben, Anne & Rainer Goldammer, Jos van der Haar, Robin Hayfield, Mark Heyburn, Felix & Topsy Hohenstein-Thun, Helen Jarvis, Ger Jonkergrouw, Diana & Benny Kanter, Zoe Laird, Mick & Delie LeMaire, Paul & Pam LeMaire, Ann and Charles MacDonald, Louise Manderson, Pascale Mathieu, John Moran, Suzy & Clive Newman, Hugh O'Neill, Graham and Jae Pratt, Fahimeh Richardson, Priscilla Spencer, Trish Stone, Robert & Maire Spencer, Paul Sullivan, Susie & John Tolhurst, Elzeline van Vulpen, Claudia Vorlaender, Aimee and Anita Van Essen, Sian Williams, Annette Willis. Also to dear Ruth Minoletti and Sally Wilson, down there in Australia.

The North American 'tribe', Bob Atkins, Lyla Berg, Elizabeth Bloom, Pia Back, Juanita Brown, Amy Broderick, Jim Burns, Jacqui Cambata, Linda Logan-Condon, Jeff Daly, Bev Davids, Sandy Fiechtner, Wink Franklin, Shakti Gawain, Maran Hendricks, Sara Hunicke, Carl & Pat Heath, Jack & Louise Hawley, David Isaacs,

Mike Iser, Tom & Karinna James, Wally & Dolores Lassen, Bob Lee, Glenn & Sharon Lehrer, Julie Leslie, Jeff Linzer, Lynne Looney, Andy Mahoney, Deborah Miller, Dani Monroe, David and Brenda Nurenberg, Marian Hudacek, Vanda Marlowe, William Miller, Jack and Kathryn Muhler, Bill Paul, Joy Peterson, Cindy and Craig Riddle, Peter Russell, Manuela Terraluna, Hinton Thomas, Michelle Tregesser, Rich and Peggy Umanzio, Frances Vaughan, Jane Winter, Theda Zaretsky, and Sam Zingaro . . . your companionship has been invaluable.

LDI companions, Mark & Katherine Yeoell, John Scherer, Sheree Jones, David Oliphant, Denise Stevens, Eugene Wyble, Chris Stahlecker, Jyo Singh, Dan Petty, Kathy Minnerly, Peter Schmidt, Mike Fuentes, Barry Gersowsky, Elaine Daigle-Kirk, Malti Karpfen, Joel Feldman . . . what an experience!

Clients and colleagues, Carlos Alavarez, Harry Andrews, John Benson, Wolfgang Boppel, Tim Coburn, Martin Coles, Paul Davies, Klaus Dieter-Hohr, Frank Ellis, Guido Engelbrecht, Pip Frankish, Wirnt Galster, Luc DeGreef, Sebastian Gilcher, George Henson, Peter Hickman, Reinhold Hiersemann, Christian Lassen, Jean Lobey, Ray Longbottom, Bob MacDonald, Catriona MacKay, Doug Mitchell, Michael Neugart, Edoardo Pieruzzi, Rosel Schneider, Jim Stake, Inge Thulin, Carl Tyer, Peter Warne, Torben Wetche, Albert Wessel, Heribert Wille, Peter Williams, Peter Wolfram, and John van Vuuren . . . you have provided a fertile field for learning.

The women of Zonta and my IWD sisters Prama Bhandari, Sarita Chawla, Maria de los Angeles Cinta, Amrita Dass, Elaine DeCanio, Ann Dosher, Gretchen Hannon, Shireen Khemchand, Rosi Lovdal, Beth Macy, Zetu Makamandela, Lupita Martinez, Leslie Mays, Marjorie Parker, Linda Pierce, Magda Rohansky, Agota Ruzsa, Lalitha Sharanund . . . I look forward to many more years of exploration together.

The Mount Shasta family, especially Gary Zukav and Linda Francis who provided a loving space in which to make my commitment to journey through the Seven Keys.

Keith Cashburn and his consciousness class of 2002–2003,

Jeannie, Gary, Christian, Claire, Pamela, Mary, Ruben, Logan, Amelle and Anthony, it's been a heart-warming and mind-blowing experience!

The South Downs Homoeopathic class of 2005, especially Shirley, Sara, Callum, Julie, Linda, Norma, Gillian, Frances, Kathy and Steve, your work is so important at this time.

The folks at EKA – Anup, Arvind, Jonathan, Ken, and Trish thanks for always being so helpful – and Amish 'Chutney' for being so mischievous.

To the next generation, Gillian & Sammie Adams, Jonathan & Rachel Adams, Alessandra, Alice and Anna Lisa Arcando, Xavier Bailey, Max Berggren, Isabel Carrasquiera, Nina Coulter, Gail & Alexina Davidson, Lucette Forbes, Dominic & Ollie Haddock, Kaohu Hee, David & Tom Kanter, Hannah Lamb, Corey Riddle, James, Paul, & Patrick Spencer; Charlotte Talbot, Amy & Guy Tolhurst, Emma Trant, Sean Yeoell, Mimosa and Savannah Love . . . you are the inspiration and the reason.

Special thanks also to Jim Garrison, the late Willis Harman, Angeles Arrien, David Whyte, His Holiness the Dalai Lama, Sri Sathya Sai Baba, and Thich Nhat Hanh . . . for your wisdom and your vision.

Thank you to John D. Adams for putting the commas where they needed to be in my life . . . and so much more. Also to Terry Mollner, who first mentioned the coming of the Relationship Age.

Finally, to Eileen Campbell, Judith Kendra and the team at Rider Books who brought this book into being – it has been a pleasure working with you.

INDEX

accountability 102–4
Adams, John D. 12, 106
addiction 42, 54, 82, 83
advocacy/enquiry balance 144–6
alliance mindset 13, 22–7, 34, 50, 61, 69, 87, 155, 192, 211, 213
  in a global society 22, 56, 186
  in organisations 25–6, 38, 87, 104, 122, 183
altruism 126
American Indians 171
anchors 73–5
anger 97–8
Arrien, Angeles 24
attachment 116–17
attraction of opposites 79–82
aura 58
authenticity 27–8
Autry, James 139

balance
  and dynamism 212
  global 89–90
  see also life balance
balanced scorecard approaches 87–8, 102
Bali bombings 77
behaviour change 145
being-doing polarity 41–2, 204
belonging 66
  global 76
Berg, Lyla 27
Berggren, Urban 87
Bertaccini, Ken 120
blame game 11, 96
bliss 180
bodily signals 158, 194
body (physical dimension) 8, 30, 57, 110
  connection with mind, spirit and emotions 31, 170
  effect of emotions 37
  self-care 70, 194
Bohm, David 145
brain hemispheres 155
breathing 118
Breton, Denise 209
Buddhism 117, 187
'bully bosses' 72
business 32
  in a global society 4, 26, 107–8
business partnerships 81, 123–4
Business Week 106, 107
butterfly metaphor 164

candle analogy 102
candour 142–3
Catford, Lorna 149
'celebration' 125
chakras 58–61
change
  containers for 164
  continuing awareness of 191
  and diversity 87–8
  facilitation 75
  and life 71
  as 'mini-death' 177
  as opportunity for growth 21–2
  as self-generating process 3
  trusting in the process 182–3
change-stability polarity 71, 198
chaos, allowing 162–3

Chawla, Sarita 140
childhood/early experience
 betrayal 112
 compliance mindset 14
 effects of rejection 50–1
 security and belonging 27, 65–6, 68
children
 imagination 152–3
 listening to 140
choice, power of 79, 215
Chopra, Deepak 204
Christianity 187
cloning 31
co-dependence 50, 51
'collective'
 care for 5
 responsibility for 23
 and security 66
collective consciousness 125, 186–7
colour 160
commitment 205–6
communication 128–9, 137
 electronic 4, 146–7, 148–9
 in organisations 139, 143
compassion 109, 114, 118, 126, 186, 201–2
complementary medicine 57, 60, 170
compliance mindset 13, 14–16, 27–8, 45, 51, 129, 199
 in organisations 15–16, 49, 55, 72, 85, 123, 197
Condon, Linda Logan 146
Connectors 8, 195, 201–4, 212
consultants 203–4
containers 164
context and meaning 199
'control junkies' 49
corporate culture 137–8
 abusive 72
cost management 16
Council of Nicea (AD 325) 176
counter-dependence 16
courage 196–7
Course in Miracles, A 173
Covey, Stephen 121
creativity 81–2, 83–4, 136
 in organisations 85
 and trust 202
creativity-reactivity polarity 207
curiosity 199
customer-centred culture 21
customers
 feelings of undervaluation 16
 loving and serving 121
 partnership orientation 25–6

Dalai Lama 34, 126
death 176–7
defiance mindset 13, 16–18, 45
dependence 14, 46, 49, 51
dialogue vs. discussion 145–6
diversity 85–7, 89, 90, 169
 change and 87–8
dreams 158–9
duality 81–2, 87
 tension and intention 210–13
Dyer, Wayne 12, 23

early experience *see* childhood
education system 27, 32, 34, 82, 187
ego 132, 139–40, 148
 and soul 14, 27–8, 52, 98, 110, 129, 131, 173, 187, 208, 209, 210
Einstein, Albert 200
electronic communication 4, 146–7, 148–9
emotions (emotional dimension) 8, 57, 110, 193–4
 connection with mind, body and spirit 31, 170
 expression of 37–40, 84, 87
 integration with mind 32–6, 136
 as movement of energy 36–40, 88
 separation from mind 30–1, 136
 vocabulary of 40
Emotional Intelligence 36, 204

emotional security 65
empowerment 103–4
energy 57–62
  in motion 36–40, 88
  and structure 197
enquiry/advocacy balance 144–6

fairness 98–9
faith 177–9
'false love' 117
fear 44–56
  of abandonment 66
  of betrayal 112
  of chaos 163
  of death 177
  destructive effects 97, 112–13
  of disapproval 94
  of failure 46–7
  of humiliation 129
  of loss of control 17, 39, 47–9, 83
  vs. love 118, 179
  of not knowing 173
  of rejection 50–2, 92
  of transformation 131
  of true knowing 154
feelings *see* emotions
feng shui 171
Fonda, Jane 168
forgiveness 109, 113, 114, 118
Fortune 500 companies 58
freedom
  and security 66–8
  truth and 131–2
Fritz, Robert 11

Gandhi, Mahatma 69, 93, 108, 126, 198
Garrison, Jim 168–9
Geller, Uri 45
generosity of spirit 112, 117
Gerber, Richard 160
Gibran, Kahlil 111, 120
global corporations 4, 42
global networks 124–5
global society 3, 4, 9, 31, 42, 58, 208
  alliance mindset 22, 56, 186
  challenges of 10–11
  establishing security 76–7
  generating passion 89–90
  honouring the mystery 185–8
  inspiring love 125–7
  sharing power 106–8
  trusting intuition 168–71
  unanswered questions 5
  voicing truth 148–50
global stewardship 26
globe hemispheres 169–70
God 111, 180
  personalised concept of 175–6
Goleman, Daniel 36, 204
Goodall, Jane 168
Gorbachev, Mikhail 168, 198
Gorbachev, Raisa 168
government 6, 31, 32, 55, 187
Greenleaf, Robert 123
guides and guardians 159
gurus 179–80

Hahn, Thich Nhat 168
hallucinogens 159
Harman, Willis 26, 154
Havel, Vaclav 61, 108,
health
  altruism and 126
  effect of emotions 37
  effects of fear in the heart 113
  self-care 70, 194
  see also stress-related disorders; illness
heart 109–10
  awakening 120–3
  integration with head 136
  opening 111–14
  separation from head 30–1, 136
hierarchical mindset 22, 101, 105
hierarchy of needs 65–6
higher intelligence 154–5, 215
Hillman, James 110

holism 23, 31, 42, 203
Houston, Jean 127
human identity 76–7
human-resources professionals 203–4
humility 148–50

identity
  and belonging 66
  human 76–7
  of true Self 92
'if somebody loses then nobody wins' 11, 22–3, 70, 155, 184, 211
illness
  absence of truth and 135–6
  energy imbalance and 60
  inhibition of spirit and 42
imagination 152–3
income differentials 106–7
independence 18, 22
Industrial Age 4
Information Age 4
inner 'knowing' 152, 155–6
inspiration 164–5
Institute of Noetic Sciences 26, 126
integrity 135–7
  in organisations 141–2
intention 208–15
interconnectedness 6–7, 31, 69, 179, 191
interdependence 23, 25–6, 124, 149
  building 104–5
Internet 4, 149, 185
intuition, trusting 59
  global implications 168–71
  organisational implications 161–7
  personal implications 151–61
intuition-logic polarity 200–1

Jonah complex 181
Jung, Carl Gustav 35, 154–5

Kennedy, John F. 165,
Khan, Pir Vilayat 80
King, Martin Luther 108, 165

Lao Tsu 211–12
Largent, Christopher 209
leadership archetypes 194–207
learning partnerships 123–4
Leider,Richard 71
Lennon, John 108, letting go 28–9
life balance 70
  value to organisations 73
listening 139–41
  Five Levels of Listening 140
love
  vs. fear 118, 179
  as only authentic power 53
love, inspiring 59
  global implications 125–7
  organisational implications 119–25
  personal implications 109–19
Luke, Hannabeth 77

MacLaine, Shirley 168
madness 156
Mandela, Nelson 53, 108
  Map Makers 8, 195, 198–201, 212
masculine/feminine energies 89
Maslow, Abraham 65–6, 181
matrix structures 101
Mbeke, Thabo 168
meditation 41, 54, 131, 156, 160, 180, 193
meetings
  candour in 144
  listening in 140
mental dimension *see* mind
mergers and acquisitions 56, 85, 88, 104, 143, 164, 203
micro-management 16, 147
'mid-life crisis' 54
mind (mental dimension) 8, 57, 110, 192–3
  connection with body, emotions and spirit 31, 170
  integration with emotions 32–6, 136
  separation from emotions 30–1, 136

mindsets 12–27
  see also alliance mindset; compliance mindset; defiance mindset; self-reliance mindset
Mitchell, Edgar 127
Mother Theresa 108
Myers Briggs Type Indicator 35, 161
Myss, Caroline 29, 53, 57–8, 136
mystery, honouring 59
  global implications 185–8
  organisational implications 181–5
  personal implications 172–81
myths *see* stories and myths

Navigators 8, 195, 204–7, 212
networks 104, 123–5
Newman, Suzy 96
non-violence 69–70
Nouwen, Henri J. M. 113–14
nuclear weapons 31
'Nuff Family' 97

Open Space 182
organisations
  alliance mindset 25–6, 38, 87, 104, 122, 183
  compliance mindset 15–16, 49, 55, 72, 85, 123, 197
  Connectors 201, 202, 203–4
  defiance mindset 17–18
  effects of inhibition of spirit 42
  emotional expression 37–40
  establishing security 72–6
  fear of failure 46–7
  fear of loss of control 49
  fear of rejection 51–2
  generating passion 85–8
  honouring the mystery 181–5
  inspiring love 119–25
  Map Makers 200, 201
  Navigators 205, 206–7
  predominance of thinking over feeling 35–6
  relationship orientation 31
  self-reliance mindset 21–2
  shadow in 55–6
  sharing power 100–6
  tension and intention 210–13
  Transformers 197, 198
  trusting intuition 161–7
  unanswered questions 5–6
  voicing truth 137–48
over-achievers 47
Owen, Harrison 182
Ozaniec, Naomi 62

Parikh, Jagdish 162
passion, generating 59
  global implications 89–90
  organisational implications 85–8
  personal implications 78–84
paternalism 49, 56, 142–3
Peck, M. Scott 92
perfectionism 48
performance health 105
personal life
  establishing security 65–72
  facing the shadow 56
  fear of loss of control 48–9
  generating passion 78–84
  honouring the mystery 172–81
  inspiring love 109–19
  sharing power 91–9
  trusting intuition 151–61
  unanswered questions 5
  voicing truth 128–37
Perspectives 127
physical dimension *see* body
physical security 65, 66
pineal gland 160
Plato 214
polarity and paradox 210–13
political politeness 15, 51, 140–1
population, global 106
position, power of 27, 93, 106, 141
possession, power of 27, 93, 106, 141
power

definitions 93–6
and fear 44–56
power, sharing 59
global implications 106–8
organisational implications 100–6
personal implications 91–9
prayer 180, 193
presence, power of 93–6, 106
project team approach 87, 101, 104
public arena 6, 15, 149
'punishment-free zones' 87
purposefulness 82–4

Ray, Michael 42, 149
reincarnation 176
Relationship Age 3–5, 6–7, 9, 22, 77, 147, 188, 191, 208
relationships
abusive 69
to divine intelligence 180
with our essence 111
and fear of loss of control 48–9
and fear of rejection 50
to groups of others 66
with our Higher Self 131
honesty in 55, 132, 143
importance in times of crisis 156
with our inner guidance 159
need for openness 19
with one another 80–1
to the Self 92
see also business partnerships; co-dependence; counter-dependence; dependence; independence; inter-dependence, sacred partnerships
religion 31, 57, 127, 150, 186, 187
resources
global inequality 106
'scarcity assumption' 11, 14, 45, 49, 150, 180
ritual 171
Rowling, J. K. 215
Russell, Peter 41
Rutigliano, Kymn Harvin 121

'sacred partnerships' 114–16
Sagan, Carl 5, 168
Saint-Exupéry, Antoine de 110
Sanchez, Oscar, Aria 168
Scherer, John 131
scientific paradigm 30–1
Seasonal Affective Disorder 160
security, establishing 59
global implications 76–7
organisational implications 72–6
personal implications 65–72
self-esteem 42, 44, 91, 94, 96, 99, 201
self-expression 128–9
self-love 110–11, 117
self-rejection 51, 92
self-reliance mindset 13, 18–22
self-sacrifice 117
Senge, Peter 162, 191
September 11 (2001) 10–11
Servant-Leadership 123
service 121–3
Seven Keys 8, 59, 61–2, 62–188
sexual expression 78–9, 80, 83
experiencing God 180
and spirituality 116
shadow 53–5, 112
sixth sense 152
Smith, Cyprian 213
'social contracts' 123–4
soul 208–10
ego and 14, 27–8, 52, 98, 110, 129, 131, 173, 187, 208, 209, 210
'soul's code' 110
soul's intention 8, 213–15
Sperry, Roger 155
spirit (spiritual dimension) 23, 30, 40–3, 57, 99, 107, 110, 193
connection with mind, body and emotions 31, 170
definition 40–1
Spiritual Renaissance 41

split-brain theory 155
State of the World Forum 168–9
Stone, Hal and Sidra 130
stories and myths
  in a global society 149
  personal 132–3
stress-related disorders 32, 37, 42, 56, 60, 70, 83
sub-personalities 130
succession vitality processes 102–3
suicide 93
Sullivan, Paul 52
support 117–18, 156
survival of the fittest 11, 14, 17, 45, 69, 184
sustainability 23, 26, 32, 76–7, 98, 107, 208
symbolism 159, 171, 200
systems perspective 31

technology 4, 185–6
Thinking and Feeling dimension 35–6
  see also emotions; mind
'three-sixty-degree' feedback 103
top-down management 46–7
Transformers 8, 195, 196–8, 212
truth, voicing 59
  global implications 148–50
  organisational implications 137–48
  personal implications 128–37
Turner, Ted 168

unanswered questions 5–7
unconditional love 8, 109, 110, 112, 118, 121, 174, 215
  in a global society 126–7
unconscious 151, 154
Universal Unconscious 154–5

Vaughan, Frances 118
visibility 74–5
vision 159
  and action 206
  global 168–9
  in organisations 21, 25, 165–6
visualisation exercises 159
voices in our head 130–1

Walsch, Neale Donald 179
Walsh, Roger 114, 117
'War for Talent' 55
wealth accumulation 14, 27, 67–8, 106, 169
WIFM ('what's in it for me?') syndrome 74
Williamson, Marianne 53
Wisdom Eye (Eye of the Heart) 213
witch burnings 153
wizardry, organisational 183–5
Wordsworth, William 110
woundedness 113–14

Yeoell, Mark 136

Zukav, Gary 46

For further information concerning Leadership Development Processes, Organisational Culture Change Processes, Workshops and Coaching based on the content of this book, please send your enquiry to: TheWisdomKeys@hotmail.com